EXTRAORDINARY
HAPPENINGS ON THE
EDGE OF LUNACY

EXTRAORDINARY HAPPENINGS ON THE EDGE OF LUNACY

*FROM LIFE-THREATENING EVENTS HE'D
WALK AWAY, FOREVER THANKFUL TO PRAY*

MR. FRANKIE PRINCETON

To order additional copies of this book, contact:
Xlibris
1-888-795-4274
www.Xlibris.com
Orders@Xlibris.com
758405

DEDICATION

I decided to write my life story and the life story of my mother because our lives affected and inspired others as we sustained, maintained, and survived, ultimately defying odds that were stacked against us. This book is written with the greatest honor, respect, and love to my mother. It is also to help others who struggle with the painful unknowns and unpredictable behaviors of mental illness.

My mother was mentally ill, but it did not manifest. She functioned in society normally and was just as normal as any one person when medication was flowing through her brain and her system, but when it was not, she behaved abnormally, and that mysterious abnormality forced me to write about it. From the start of her battle with mental illness until her death, my mother's diagnosis was incorrect. I believe there's no way for a doctor to really form a prognosis for a mentally ill patient because after diagnosis, the patient's mind fights, changes, and adapts to the degenerating and aging brain, the different types of medications, the lack of brain exercise, and the effects of life-altering habits like smoking. Our family endured and labored a lot because of [or owing to] the parents' negligence, the entire family suffered. We did not receive important information on how to truly help our mother. For years, our mother was diagnosed by several doctors as having bipolar disorder, but she also had schizophrenia and delusion occurring in conjunction with paranoia, insecurities, sleep deprivation, isolation, mistrust, and lots of suspicions. Mom was constantly changing medications over the years because of having several different doctors who didn't take the time to find out what disorder she really had. They took professional and educated guesses. Some medications worked for a while and then stopped because her mind and body was changing as well. It was hard to pinpoint exactly what medication would work for her.

Four years after Mom died, I found a disorder that fit her exactly, but it still was not all that Mom suffered from. The main disorder that I found after Mom died was paranoid personality disorder. If doctors had known this disorder and pinned it to Mom, she probably could and would have lived a more normal life. By my accounts, Mom had paranoid personality disorder with bipolar disorder, schizophrenia, insecurities, and isolation. I don't recall Mom being depressed even in the slightest.

This book is mainly about the life of my mother and me. There are still stories from my two sisters and two brothers that need to be told when and if we collaborate. The family had to endure and deal with multiple burnings, Black Panther encounters, a car door being opened while driving, a near-fight with Angela Davis, a stabbing, an incident of being sprayed with Mace, the killing of a cow, an incident of urinating on a Bible, and so on. People will wonder why the kids in our family never received counseling. The telling of this story is so you can get some advice, ideas, and ways to help a loved one with a mental illness. Anyone with a mental illness will always be known as a loved one to me. Our loved one, our mother, lived an unusual life filled with so much pain, and she had a lot of unasked and unanswered questions. I think of the way she lived her life as someone walking in the dark. When you walk in darkness, you walk either quietly or loudly. A person walks quietly because they are afraid, and they use their sense of hearing to listen their way out of the darkness so as not to alert or disturb anyone. A person walking loudly in the darkness hopes someone will come to their rescue or assist them. Most times, it's best to be heard rather than seen, so you can get the help you need.

When you are a little four-year-old girl who has just been moved to a different household with people you barely know even though they are your relatives, it can be very frightening and can put you in a state of shock. At the age of four, you are starting to understand love from your parents expressing it to you. Love shapes your thinking, and love nurtures your emotions in both your brain and heart because they are closely linked together. Mom's heart did develop love naturally and normally over the years because she instilled and expressed love to me and my siblings growing up, but her brain's development was blocked and/or infected with mixed signals in ways that we never understood, and that infection revealed itself in the form of a mental illness. Right when she was understanding love, the teaching process suddenly stopped, and the love she was taught after that got misconstrued. The little bit of love in her heart that she got from her mother remained, but that same little bit of love in her brain metamorphosed, and the results of that metamorphosis is what you will read within this book. What I am saying is only a hypothesis of mine, and that is the closest I can begin to understand what happened to my mother. I pray that after you finish reading this book, you will be inspired and grow to love my mother, if not more than I do.

DEFINITIONS AND REASON

At the beginning of writing this life story, I came up with several different titles before I settled on one. One of the titles I had was *Mind's Maze* because I was so amazed at how Mother's mind functioned. My mother's mind had me perplexed and scratching my head, wondering why she was not 100 percent right, so I wrote a few definitions for *mind* and *maze* to help me understand the perplexity of those words. But even after reading them, I had no more understanding than where I started. Trying to understand my mother's mental condition simply amazed me for years and still amazes me now that she is gone. I believe her mind will amaze you too.

The Google definition of *maze* is "a network of paths and hedges designed as a puzzle through which one has to find a way."

From Merriam-Webster, it is "(1) a complex network of paths or passages, especially one with high hedges in a garden, designed to puzzle those walking through it, comparable to *labyrinth*; (2) a similar system represented diagrammatically as a pattern of lines; or (3) any confusing network of streets, pathways, etc.: a maze of paths.

The Free Dictionary:

a. An intricate, usually confusing network of interconnecting pathways, as in a garden; a labyrinth.
b. A physical situation in which it is easy to get lost.

The Google definition of *mind*:

1. The element of a person that enables them to be aware of the world and their experiences, to think and to feel; the faculty of consciousness and thought
2. A person's intellect

From Merriam-Webster:

1. The element or complex of elements in an individual that feels, perceives, thinks, wills, and especially reasons
2. The conscious mental events and capabilities in an organism

I wanted to give some definitions just in case you weren't sure of their meanings. A maze can be very complex, and if you are not 100 percent focused, you will be lost or at a loss for words on how to figure it out. One wrong move or slight deviation in your understanding could take you to a path that confuses you more. And since most people look at the mind from the outside in, it can be hard to understand. The mind is still not fully understood by medical experts because of its complexity. The mind can be altered in ways that will perplex the smartest of smart people.

Drugs, whether over the counter at your friendly neighborhood drugstore or cooked over someone's stove, can alter your mind for an undetermined time, even permanently. The mind itself is already a maze, and drugs complexes it even more. Drugs can open the mind to thoughts, ideas, visions, and behaviors beyond the usual. Prescribed drugs by your family or walk-in pharmacist are designed to alter the mind so that you can function in your everyday life. Drugs will work for a certain amount of time before their effects wear off, and you must ingest more so you can maintain your level of functionality or cognitive abilities. Prescribed drugs and over-the-counter drugs must be taken to their exact directions for them to work as intended. You cannot deviate from the directions, or you will cause harm to yourself or others. Prescribed and OTC drugs can be good as a remedy because they help and assist many. Administering them correctly for the mentally ill is extremely important to protect the public in general because these drugs help mentally ill people interact with the general population on an everyday, manageable level. A prescription of medication could mean taking tablets, a liquid dose, an intravenous application, or a shot in the buttocks—which can make a tremendous difference to a mentally ill person simply because shots react quicker. Drugs can be taken negatively and positively, and we must help one another to take them correctly.

Now let me speak on the terms *mentally ill* and *mentally challenged*. Both *ill* and *challenged* coming after *mentally* sounds deficient, weak, and ugly and causes a major problem for me. The terms *mentally ill* and *mentally challenged* should be changed worldwide to *mentally brave*. The definition of *brave* is "ready to face and endure danger or pain; showing courage." The verb definition of *brave* says "endure or face (unpleasant conditions or behavior) without showing fear." The mentally brave show great bravery every day because they don't know what to expect on any new day. The mentally brave face things differently than the average person. They are already brave within themselves because of their deficiency, and then they have to deal with prejudice, discrimination, and being misunderstood, threatened, made fun of, stared at, and not being given a helping hand except by those closest to them. Why would we not call them brave? I consider myself a normal person, but some days I must mentally prepare myself to enter society, and it can be scary at times. Some days I keep up a certain image, a façade, a pose, a smile, or a frown, or I keep quiet to fit in so as not to be teased and be the brunt of a joke. It can be overwhelming at times, so I watch my back, my front, and my comings and goings. It can be so perplexing that I wish I have some of the bravery that the *mentally brave* have.

And while I am on the subject, the mentally brave terminology should be more defined in describing the mentally brave as everyday law-abiding citizens who hold jobs successfully, have beautiful families, have wonderful, grateful friends, and have beautiful, loyal pets. And then there are the ones who commit crimes, break the law, and hurt other people in our society who should be descriptively called mentally ill. We can no longer talk about the mentally ill as one person. My mother held a job with the Postal Service for over fifteen years successfully, and she did not physically harm anyone. She was kind and well liked and loved by many, and she is the reason I am writing this book. My dear, loving mother was so brave on many levels. She was courageous beyond my comprehension, and she was brave up until she died at the age of seventy. For my mother to go through what she went through and have a strong desire to live up to seventy is amazing to me. She never wanted to take her own life or even spoke of shortening her life. You will be amazed when you read our story, and you will grow to love my mother as much as I did. I hope you enjoy the insight and the message.

CHAPTER ONE

A prelude and my theory; Dad is stationed at Fort Riley, Kansas, and we live in Junction City from 1963 to 1966; Mom has her first mental illness incident

A beautiful and rambunctious little four-year-old Amanda is playing in the living room when her dad Big John Vance comes home after an agonizing day at work that was filled with teasing, taunting, and revealing information about his wife. Big John opens the front door to his house and sees his only daughter, and little Amanda is extremely excited to see her father. She runs over to him and jumps into his arms, and he gives her a big hug and kisses her on the forehead. He looks her into her eyes and then puts her down and tells her he loves her very much. Little Amanda is so excited because her daddy, whom she loved dearly, is home, but her excitement would quickly turn into despair and uncertainty. He then walks to the bedroom where his wife Catherine is. Big John and Catherine start to argue, and the arguing intensifies and becomes violent. Little Amanda runs to her room and grabs her favorite toy, which is a green stuffed turtle, and she clasps on to it ever so tightly as she balls up into the closet as if she has heard them argue before. Amanda can now hear furniture being tossed around and numerous perfume bottles clinking together as they are broken into tiny pieces. The yelling and screaming between the two of them gets louder and louder, and then suddenly, she hears

1

Catherine getting slapped. Big John has slapped Catherine and sends her across the room, and Amanda can hear her mother hitting the floor as if she herself has been thrown there.

Little Amanda was terrified but wanted to go see her parents, so she worked up the nerve and very slowly walked toward her parents' room. As she got closer, she heard her mother yell, "No, Big John, please don't, please, not my baby!" Right when little Amanda was just feet outside her parents' bedroom door, she heard a gunshot. She heard her mother say really quietly as if she was in a state of shock, "Oh my god," and then she heard a second shot, and it was completely quiet. A minute later, she heard a third shot and a big thud hitting the bedroom floor. Little Amanda just sat down outside her parents' door, waiting and hugging her stuffed turtle oh so tightly. "Daddy, Momma, Doug, Daddy, Momma, Doug," she called. She waited there just like she had many times before because she was instructed not to enter her parents' bedroom without permission. A neighbor must have heard the gunshots coming from inside the house because he went over to see what happened. The neighbor knocked on the door, but there was no answer, so he walked in. He walked cautiously and slowly until he made it to the bedroom and saw little Amanda sitting outside. The neighbor walked into the bedroom and was shocked at what he saw. He slowly walked backward out of the bedroom, grabbed little Amanda, took her to their house, and called the authorities. The police later concluded that in the later part of spring 1946, Big John Vance committed double homicide/suicide, killing his wife, son, and himself. Through investigation, they learned that Big John Vance had always suspected that his wife was seeing other men and received knowledge at work that the little boy was not his. Big John lost his sense of reality. Almost immediately, little Amanda would go live with her aunt and uncle. Months later, little Amanda would be adopted by her aunt and uncle, and they would receive financial assistance to care for her.

Amanda is now in her twenties and is married as I begin to tell the story. The furthest back I can remember about my life is when I was maybe two years old. I remember my aunt sitting me on her white six-drawer bedroom dresser with a big beautiful mirror. She had a man standing on the other side of it. I believe I was around the age of ten when I began to look back at my earliest memories. I thought it was amazing to be able to remember so many things and events in my life that happened when I was just a small tike. I was around fifteen when I started to really care about recalling all the memories and events that happened in my life. That was one of the reasons I wrote this book—I felt like I could remember things very well and wanted to do so before I lost the ability to recall as I got older.

Let me start from the beginning of our family. My dad lived in a town southeast of Dallas, Texas, called West Daytona, and he graduated from West Daytona High as a star basketball player. My mother lived eight miles away in Dolphin, and she attended the same high school as Dad. The two met, courted, and soon married. Mom got pregnant at the age of sixteen and gave birth to my oldest brother Wayne in 1959. After Dad graduated from high school, he wanted to live in West Daytona with his wife and son, but Mom didn't want to live there nor live in Dolphin, so she strongly encouraged him to move. Dad had some family living in Los Angeles, so he moved the family there, and that was where I was born in 1961. Farrah, my sister, would also be born in Los Angeles in 1962. Dad was quite busy at his young age.

Living in Los Angeles would not last long because Dad was drafted into the army and had to leave for Fort Conquest, Louisiana, to do his basic training. Dad's family couldn't go with him to basic training, so we remained in Los Angeles. Once he finished basic training, he received papers for his first duty station of Fort Riley, Kansas. Dad found the family a house in Junction City, and that is where my first memories of Mom's mental illness are set, as well as my first Christmas. We lived in Kansas from 1963 to 1966.

One day our mother took me, my oldest brother Wayne, and Farrah on the city bus to go downtown, but on the way back home, we had an unusual encounter with Santa Claus. All that I remember is that the encounter escalated negatively into a shouting match. The bus came to our neighborhood stop, and we exited and began to walk home, and as we got closer to home, Wayne and I ran to play in the front yard so we could make snow angels and a snowman because it had snowed a lot that day. Dad told me that he watched us walk home from the front porch and saw that Mom was walking slowly as large pieces of snowflakes landed on her. Dad thought that incident was strange because the lady Mom was walking with ran to our house because the snowflakes were falling so hard and fast. Shortly after that, Dad had to put Mom in the hospital because of her strange behavior.

Now that I look back on that one incident forty years later, I remember it slightly different. On that day, I remember playing outside in the snow and Mom coming outside and standing on the front porch to check on me. When Mom called my name and I turned to look at her to answer, suddenly, a large avalanche of snow slid off the front of the roof and fell on her. The next thing I remember is that she was in the hospital. That is my first memory of Mom getting sick. Dad used to tell us that Mom was sick, and for the longest time, that was what we called it—sick. Sick was another way of saying Mom was having her mental breakdowns, but as we got older and Mom was being put in the hospital more often, we started calling her sickness as nervous breakdowns because that was what the doctors told Dad.

Sometime before that snow falling accident, my dad had dressed up as Santa Claus, or I thought it was Dad. Some forty years later, I asked him if he dressed up as Santa Claus, and he said that he didn't. On the night in question, Wayne and I were taking a bath, and Dad had gone outside, probably to take the trash out. The next thing I remember is seeing Santa Claus at the living room window. It was terrifying for me to see a white-bearded, bright-red-suited Santa Claus at my age. It could have been a neighbor or a prankster, but all these years I thought it was Dad. A few days passed by, and for the first time, our grandmother came to live with us for a little while because Mom was in the hospital and someone needed to care for me, Wayne, and Farrah. Our grandmother was not actually our grandmother but really our great-aunt Lacy Deal. She was Mom's aunt and was given the responsibility of raising Mom. For many years, I believed she was my grandmother, and we were told to call her Nana. Her husband was Peter Deal Sr., and I knew him as my grandfather, but he was really my great-uncle. We were told to call him Big Pa. The reason Peter and Lacy Deal were responsible for raising my mother was that her biological parents died when she was four years old. That incident was the core and root of my mother's mental illness and state of mind.

My mother dealt with an awful lot of dramatic and traumatic incidents at a very young age. She also had a brother, but he died when he was two years of age. She remembered her brother very well and spoke of him to me a lot. Her brother's death affected her strongly even though she was four years old when she lost him. She loved and missed him and never got over it. She said often to me that she wished she had brothers and sisters growing up. She would talk about having siblings and how that would have helped her through life because she felt so alone quite often. That was one of the reasons she wanted to have a lot of kids—we wouldn't be alone in this world. Her brother died right before the next traumatic incident in her life, still at the age of four. As I ponder the chain of events in Mom's childhood, my thoughts consider other scenarios about the death of Mom's brother. I do not know the cause of his death, but I wonder if it was an accident or if it was caused by someone or an illness. It is in my theory at the beginning of the book.

Mom's next tragic incident would be more traumatic than losing her brother and would forever change her life. Through historical research by my siblings, they found out that Mom most likely witnessed her father killing his wife, her mother, and then killing himself in an apparent murder/suicide. That tragedy altered my mother's life at the age of four, which brings me back to the death of my mother's brother. It may have been at the hands of their father. I do not know the full story of that incident because it was hard to get details, and the incident was kept from us siblings. Sometime in my late twenties, I started asking questions about my mother's past from various family members on my mother's side, and I received information that would help me understand the circumstances surrounding my grandparents' deaths. At the same time, they would leave me speechless and puzzled.

Early on in my life, I was told that my mother's father who committed the murder/suicide was not my mother's biological father. And I was told that my mother's mother fooled around a lot, and her husband supposedly found out and killed her and then himself.

5

This brings me to believe that my mother's supposed father may have believed that my mother's brother was not his child and killed him as well, which would probably have been even more reason for him to kill himself. From some of the talks I have had with my mother, I've learned that she did not receive much help as a little girl in dealing with the enormous loss of her immediate family. Mom told me that she was instructed not to talk about it and to keep quiet and not ask questions even with the little bit of information she did know. I was made to draw my own conclusion that there was not much help and assistance back in 1946 for an impoverished farm cropper and his housewife, like my great-uncle Peter Deal Sr. and great-aunt Lacy Deal who were raising my mother. I was told that they did receive money from the state to care for Mom. And let me mention that they were a black family living in the Deep South of Texas, in Dolphin. And back in that day, black families had their way of dealing with the day-to-day affairs of accidents and problems. Now, looking back at it from that perspective, my mother was at the mercy of Almighty God and her aunt and uncle. As my mother told me, she received plenty of nurturing, support, and love from her aunt and uncle. She said she felt real secure with the love and support that her uncle Peter Deal Sr. gave to her.

Mom told me that things changed once her aunt and uncle had children of their own, namely Rachel Fay, Peter Jr. (Pete), and Layla Deal. For a while, Mom believed they were her own brother and sisters. Mom said she was not receiving as much attention as she once was because of the addition of her foster brother and sisters, but actually, they were her cousins. Mom said her aunt treated her more sternly and gave her more rules, chores, and responsibilities than her cousins. As she got older, her relationship with her uncle was not as strong as it used to be, but he still showed care and fairness toward her. I am not sure at what age Mom was told the story of her parents' tragic demise, but it had to be painful until she was told the truth, which probably increased the pain and suffering.

I believe I was around the age of thirteen when I started hearing about my mother's mother. I wasn't confused, but from time to time, I would ponder about my mother's mother, my real grandma. To this day, I wonder why I was not told about the family tree. I guess my own parents probably just felt like I knew or understood the ancestry, but I was just a very immature and clueless teenager. Had I known what a family tree was, I probably would have asked more questions about who my grandparents were, and even asked about the simple fact that I had two sets of grandparents—one on my mother's side and one on my father's side. When I was finally shown a picture of my mother's mother, it never occurred to me at that time to ask questions about her. To this day, I do not know why I/we were not told of the tragedy of our grandparents and the circumstances surrounding their deaths.

CHAPTER TWO

A very short concrete history of mental illness medication; our family's first burning

L ife, a whirlwind of make-believe events until it really hits home in the form of a tragedy or a memorable celebration. I began to understand that life was not make-believe and fantasy at a young age. It was very eccentric for me by the time I was six years old. One of the first things I really remember in my life is my father wearing an army uniform and getting ready to leave for work. I remember lying in bed getting ready to go to sleep and Dad reaching over to kiss me goodnight and say goodbye. Wayne was in bed with me, but I can't remember if Dad kissed him goodbye or not.

The next thing I recall is the incident that would change my life forever. For over forty years, I believed that snow from the roof of our house slid off and fell on my mother when we lived in Junction City, Kansas, and that she had a lengthy stay in the hospital for it. I came to believe that was the very first incident in Mom's mental illness battle. But as I think about it now, Mom's visit to the emergency room that evening may have triggered, released, or opened a dormant deficiency in her brain. I am most sure if the doctors administered medications to my mother, the medications may very well have hurt her more than helped her because the doctors didn't know my mother's medical history. She didn't even have a proper diagnosis early on in her life. With the use of medications still evolving and in its early stages back in 1965, physicians probably still knew very little about the side effects of combining different types of medications. Also, the way medication was administered back in 1965 to black Americans was different. They were not treated equally and fairly like white Americans and were given generic and cheaper drugs. It sounds like Ritalin was widely used back then, but Dad told me that Thorazine was prescribed to my mother. I did some research throughout the Internet looking for answers and came across this excerpt: **http:// www.cesar.umd.edu/cesar/drugs/ritalin.asp**

Ritalin

Profile

Methylphenidate, brand name Ritalin, is an amphetamine-like central nervous system stimulant used to treat attention-deficit hyperactivity disorder (ADHD) in children, adolescents, and adults, as well as narcolepsy.[1] It is a Schedule II controlled substance.[2]

Ritalin is just one brand name for methylphenidate. Sustained- or extended-release formulas of methylphenidate are sold as Ritalin SR, Ritalin LA, Metadate ER, Metadate CD, Methylin ER, and Concerta.[3]

History

First synthesized in 1944, the Ritalin formula (at that time commonly known as MPH, from methylphenidate) was improved in 1950, and by 1954 it was being tested on humans. In 1957, Ciba Pharmaceutical Company began marketing MPH as Ritalin to treat chronic fatigue, depression, psychosis associated with depression, narcolepsy, and to offset the sedating effects of other medications. It was used into the 1960s to try to counteract the symptoms of barbiturate overdose. For a period, MPH was sold in combination with other products, particularly a tonic of MPH, hormones and vitamins, marketed as Ritonic in 1960, intended to improve mood and maintain vitality. [4]

9

Research on the therapeutic value of Ritalin began in the 1950s, and by the 1960s, interest focused on the treatment of "hyperkinetic syndrome," which would eventually be called Attention Deficit Hyperactivity Disorder.[5] In the United States, the use of Ritalin and other stimulants to treat ADHD steadily increased in the 1970s and early 80s, but between 1991 and 1999, Ritalin sales in the United States increased 500 percent.[6,7] The United Nations reports that the United States produces and consumes as much as 85 percent of the worlds production of Ritalin.[8]

From Stahl's Essential Psychopharmacology, Neuroscientific Basis and Practical, "Thorazine (chlorpromazine) was the first drug developed with specific antipsychotic action and would serve as the prototype for the phenothiazine class of drugs, which later grew to comprises several other agents." I am sure that when my mother went to the hospital to be treated from the snow-falling incident, she showed some signs that warranted the doctors to prescribe her either Thorazine or Ritalin. From my dad's firsthand accounts, Mom used Thorazine for many years, and its effects didn't work effectively or positively, nor did she really get better. She fought the mental illness battle most of her life, and it got worse up until she passed away.

I don't know anything about her early years between four and sixteen years of age. When Mom was admitted into the hospital for the snow-falling incident, I guess her condition was worse than some thought, as she stayed in the hospital longer than expected. I thought and believed for many years that the incident was only because of the snow falling on her, but that was probably the first nervous breakdown she had because Dad never spoke of any behavioral concerns prior to that. Our great-aunt Nana, who we thought for years was our grandmother, came to stay and take care of me, Wayne, and Farrah. She had traveled from the south of Dolphin, Texas, and it would be her last time to ever travel from her home to help Dad with Mom and us. One day Nana decided to make herself some coffee because she loved her coffee, and back then, the water was boiled on the stove in an old-fashioned metal coffee pot. When the coffee was ready, it made a loud whistling sound that got the curiosity of us kids. Nana poured herself a very hot cup of coffee and sat it on the edge of the kitchen table. My sister Farrah must have been really curious, as she went to see what was in Nana's steaming hot cup, getting really close to the kitchen table. Before anyone could tell her to get away from the cup of coffee on the table, Farrah reached up and pulled the cup to herself. Farrah immediately screamed out loud and took off running throughout the house like someone was trying to murder her. The hot coffee burned Farrah's stomach. Nana caught Farrah at some point and settled her down a little. Farrah cried and cried and was in miserable pain. I saw the burn on Farrah's stomach before bandages were applied, and it was darn gruesome—the hot coffee had peeled away Farrah's skin and left a scar that was red like blood, but it wasn't bleeding. The scar was in the shape of an "S" and covered most of Farrah's abdominal area. Farrah was rushed to the hospital for her burns. I remember seeing the white bandages that had been applied to cover the burn on Farrah's stomach. Nana had to change the dressings often. The whole ordeal had to be pretty dramatic, overwhelming, and exhausting for Nana, not to mention Farrah was probably hysterical and uncomfortable in every way.

Nana was only expecting to care for three little children, relax, and enjoy being away from her home like a mini vacation, but it didn't turn out that way. She had to bear the burden of dealing with Mom's mental state and now Farrah's burn that she probably felt completely responsible for. Nana was already away from her own three children and husband. Plus, she was in a town she was not familiar with at all. The whole thing had to be overwhelming for her. Farrah would eventually heal, Mom would come home, and Nana would go back to her family. Her experience and visit with us was not a good one and probably was a deciding factor in her not coming to help again.

CHAPTER THREE

*Dad is stationed at Fort Lewis, and we live in Tacoma,
Washington, from June 1966 to 1969; our family has its
second major burning; a real angel introduces itself to me
from the closet; my second grade teacher abuses me*

I t is June 1966, and Dad is ordered to move to Washington to an
army base named Fort Lewis where he would be stationed. Dad
finds a house for the family in Tacoma. That was where I first
attended school, in preschool. I remember going to preschool, first, and
second grades. My first grade teacher was Mrs. Lawson, and she was a
great teacher. She was an old lady in her fifties, and I really liked her.
I used to walk home from school by myself, and I was not sure how or
why my parents would let me, but they did. I wasn't scared until one
day, I got lost walking home from school. I thought I knew my way
back home because I had been shown the way many times, but I still
couldn't remember. I wasn't really lost because our house was right
across the street from where I ended up at, a neighbor's house. I didn't
realize that our house was just across the street. I went to a random
house when I couldn't find ours. Mom had written our home phone
number on the inside of my lunch pail. The neighbors saw the phone
number and called my mom, and she told them where we lived, and it
was right across the street. All I had to do was turn ninety degrees and
walk home. I was so happy and glad to see Mom.

Tacoma, Washington, was a wonderful place to live in mainly because it was the place where I first learned the love of my life—fishing. Fishing was so rewarding to me, and I just truly loved it. I loved fishing so much that I thought that when I died, I wanted to come back as a fish of some kind. My love for fish grew so strong that the first time I saw the Miami Dolphins logo, I fell in love with the team. But back to my mother. She was quite stable in Tacoma, or at least it seemed that way to me. I believe Mom was most stable there than in any other place in her life, and she was the strongest when we lived in San Fernando Valley, California, when Velvet was born in 1969. I didn't notice anything out of the norm. After that snow-falling accident in Kansas, I had grown to really pay attention to Mom and her behavior. My youngest brother Ross was born in Washington on July 17, 1966, and no one could have predicted the future, but there would be another major accident. Well, I would say it was probably around April 1967 because Ross was crawling at that time, which would have made him about eight months old. Well one day, my mother was cleaning the refrigerator and defrosting the freezer. For all you Deep South people, when the top section of the refrigerator, namely the freezer, needed to be defrosted because there was so much ice buildup, a large pot of scalding hot water would be placed inside the freezer to speed up the ice-melting process. Just as Mom was placing the pot of water in the freezer to melt the ice, Ross crawled into the kitchen and was at my mother's feet. She was so glad to see him make his way into the kitchen with his big beautiful smile. Without realizing it, my mother reached down to move Ross so he wouldn't get hurt in case she accidently spilled some hot water, but as soon as Mom went to pick Ross up, the scalding hot pot of water made the ice buildup turn very slippery. The pot began to slide out of the freezer without Mom knowing it, and it fell right on her right foot. Ross was not harmed in the incident. Mom screamed and hollered and was hysterical. She screamed out to my dad, and he ran into the house and saw Mom's foot. It was red just above the ankle down, and steam was oozing off her foot.

Once again, Mom had to be rushed to the hospital, and only God knows what kind of medication the doctors gave her to calm down.

I was most sure Mom remained hysterical and out of control. The doctors may have been unaware of any medications she was already taking and probably prescribed her something that counteracted them. But if Dad was on his game, and most of the time he was, I am sure he gave the doctors information about the medications she may have been taking currently or had taken in the past. Back in the late 1960s, medical record-keeping for military families probably was sufficient. I hope they had a good system, since military families moved so often, and their medical records followed them from hospital to hospital in a timely manner. Medical records were different then—a kid's shot was recorded where they were prepared, and the document was given to the parent for safekeeping and immediate access. Medical records were different, especially military medical records, because most contained material needed to be kept confidential for a family's security. I assume the doctors did the best they could to help Mom back then. Mom would eventually come home wearing a white bandage that completely covered her foot, ankle, and went halfway up her shin. It would take months for Mom to heal completely and walk on that foot, but I could tell that she still had severe pain, and I was most sure she was prescribed some form of painkillers. She experienced different levels of pain, and she would rub some soothing ointment on that foot as it began to heal. There were many times when I would rub that soothing ointment on my mother's foot. I would even lay my face and head on Mom's feet to comfort her. I would do this almost every day to help her get through that ordeal with as much comfort and ease as possible. That random act of love and kindness I did for my mother secured our relationship for the rest of our lives.

Mom treat me much differently from the others because I showed genuine care for her. My siblings displayed care and concern for Mom too, but she used to tell me that Dad used to get upset with her for treating me differently from the others. For all I know, Mom may have spoken to each one of us individually at separate times and told us all the same thing, which reminds me of a scene in the movie *The Prince of Tides* starring Barbara Streisand and Nick Nolte—which should have won an Oscar for best picture the year it came out. In the scene, Nick

Nolte is narrating the story of his mother calling him into her bedroom and telling him he was the best kid out of the three of them and that the others would not amount up to much. She told him to keep it a secret from his siblings. As Nick Nolte talked with his psychiatrist, who was Barbara Streisand, he told her that when he and his siblings grew older, they all said that their mother brought each one of them into her room and told them all the same thing, and he and his siblings laughed about that. That scene reminded me of my mother. I don't know if she did that to each of us because we never thought or spoke of anything like that.

Dad was not around very much mainly because he was doing a lot of army things—at least it seemed that way to me. We kids were left to be on our own a good amount of time, but thank God we didn't get into a lot of trouble or mischief. One time my brother Wayne and I went fishing with about four of our friends. We went fishing in a small lake that was located about a half mile from our house, which was located just inside the woods. Out of all the kids, I was the best fisherperson because I took fishing very seriously. We started fishing in the early afternoon and finished when it turned pitch dark. Fishing on that wonderful day was great for everyone because they were catching rainbow trout, but I was not catching anything, not a single fish. We were all using corn that day, and the rainbow trout were feeding like there was no tomorrow. I don't know why I was not catching fish, but since I was not catching fish, I decided to catch tadpoles. The tadpoles were very easy to catch because they were fat and plump. I loved seeing the jellylike eggs of the frogs all clustered together. It was so cool. Well, the gang had caught about twenty or thirty rainbow trout that day, but I hadn't caught one. But right before we quit fishing, and to my extreme excitement, I finally hooked into a fish—a big rainbow, the biggest one out of all the fish. I was so proud and felt like a king, and everyone was amazed.

But what we didn't know was that my mom, the other mothers, and the whole neighborhood were looking for us. As we approached my house, Mom and the other moms greeted us in anger and worry. Mom was so mad that she made me and Wayne walk back down to the lake in the darkness and throw all the fish back into the water. Mom probably made us throw the fish back because she knew she would be the one cleaning all those damn fish because Dad hadn't taught Wayne and me how to clean fish yet. Wayne and I walked back to the lake, but we couldn't see the lake because it was so dark, and I didn't know if we even came close to the water when we threw the fish. I went back home and was so heartbroken because I had spent all that time fishing and only catching one, the biggest one of the day. Mom punished us, and we couldn't go anywhere beyond the yard for about a week.

A few days passed by, and the whole family went to the store. On the way home, we passed by a lake I had not seen before. My eyes burst wide open when I saw the lake, and to me, it was glowing with patches of fog all around, and I felt like it was calling my name. I could not wait until the weekend so I could go fishing there. The weekend came, and I got up early in the morning, got together what little gear I had, and got ready to walk to the lake. Mom must have heard me rustling around because she called me to her room. She asked me what I was doing, and I told her I was getting ready to go fishing. She told me I could not because I was still under punishment. She then made me lay down on the floor at the foot of her bed. I was so heartbroken, and I cried myself to sleep, having never fished in that lake. Since Wayne and I were still under punishment and couldn't go fishing, we decided to go walk around the lake because Mom didn't say we couldn't do that. As we walked around the lake, we saw lots of big bullfrogs in and out of the water. As we got closer to them, they would leap high and then into the water. Well, we walked up to one that was huge and was barely in the water. Wayne and I decided that we would throw rocks at it to capture it. Wayne stood closest to the bullfrog, and I was behind him just up the incline on the embankment. We made a decision that on the count of three, we would throw our rocks to try to hit the bullfrog. We started the countdown, and on three, we threw our rocks. I quickly jumped with excitement because I knew I hit the bullfrog. I looked into the water and didn't see the bullfrog, and then I turned to look at Wayne, and he was slumped over, holding his head.

I asked him, "What's wrong? What happened?"

He said, "You hit me in the back of my head."

I said, "Really? Oh I am so sorry."

Wayne's head was bleeding badly, so we ran home to show Mom. She was mad at us for disobeying her and going to the lake. Mom patched up Wayne's gash and put us back under punishment. Some time passed, and we were taken off punishment, and one evening, while I was playing outside, my nose started bleeding. It was the first time I remember my nose ever bleeding, and from then on it would happen regularly well into my mid-twenties. As an eight-year-old boy, I didn't know why my nose would bleed without warning, and my mom had no explanation to give me either. Later in life, I would think that maybe my nose bled because the room was dry, but that time I was outside. I didn't know how to handle nosebleeds, and when it first happened that day, it bled an awful lot, and I was afraid to tell Mom for I thought she would get mad at me and make me come into the house. The bad thing about me having that first nosebleed is that I swallowed my blood. I used to think that swallowing the blood would help me because I was putting the blood back into my own body, plus it sort of tasted good. Apparently, that one day, I swallowed too much of my own blood, and soon my body started rejecting it. My stomach hurt really bad, and I started feeling sick. Well, I told Mom, and she took me to the bathroom. Mom drew me a warm bath, thinking that it would settle my stomach. After I got in the tub, I vomited up all that blood into the bathtub. The amount of blood filled the bottom of the tub—or it seemed that way from the sight of an eight-year-old kid. I hadn't seen so much blood before, and I think it scared my mom, but she never took me to the hospital. She told me that I should not swallow my own blood, and we all eventually went to bed for the night.

On that same night, a strange thing happened. Wayne and I slept in one bed together while my sister Farrah slept in a separate bed by herself, but all three of us were in the same bedroom. Late that same night, I woke up but remained in the bed. I looked toward the hallway just beyond the foot of our bed. Wayne slept on the side of the bed up against the wall, and I slept on the side where we would enter and exit the bed. There was a door that I could see in the hallway because Mom would leave a light on in the hallway. As I lay there staring at the door, it opened very slowly, and then suddenly, a blurry figure shaped like a person emerged through the door. The blurry figure started coming toward me very slowly. I was in a state of shock and could not move, scream, or say anything. As the blurry figure got closer, I saw that it was unrecognizable, but it did have a face. The figure got so close to me that its face was just inches away from mine. It stared at me for about fifteen seconds, and then it went back to the closet where it came from. A few seconds after it was back in the closet, I could move again. I never saw the blurry figure ever again. I told my mother the next morning, but she didn't believe me. She told me that I was dreaming, but I know I did not dream that. To this day, I believe it was an angel from God coming to say it would protect me and that it would be taking care of Mom all the days of our lives.

On an odd night, days and weeks later, something happened, and it was very different from the blurry figure coming out of the closet. Something very naughty happened after we were all put to bed. The three of us were still sleeping in the same bedroom. Well that night, I overheard my brother Wayne and my sister Farrah talking about how they wanted to see each other's private parts. Once again, I was in shock but a different kind of shock, and I said to myself, "Oowie, private parts." But I remained quiet and pretended to be asleep because I knew I was not going to participate in this act. I can't tell you why I did not participate and just join them, other than I remembered how Mom had taught us to not look or mess with one another's private parts. I just wasn't that kind of kid to be curious about something like that. Wayne and Farrah agreed to look at each other's private parts. I saw Farrah stand up on her bed, and then Wayne get out from under the sheets and crawl to the end of the bed on his hands and knees so that he could get a good look at Farrah's private parts. I saw Farrah pull down her panties, but right at that moment, I pulled the covers over my head because I didn't want to look.

School was very close to our house, so Wayne and I would walk to and from school, and one day in the second grade, I was walking home by myself. I am not sure why Wayne was not with me, but on that day, as I got closer to my neighborhood, I saw a drunk old man sitting on a large rock just inside an area of tall grass. I asked the drunk old man what he was doing, and he said to me, "Little guy, never drink alcohol and never do drugs because it will ruin your life." I walked away and never saw that man ever again. Maybe he was that angel visiting me again. I was only in the second grade at that time, but those wise words never left me. I never used drugs and never became a drunkard. I tell that same story to my own kids and to the kids in school where I work as often as I can.

Now on a separate day, while walking home from school, this car with two white men in it passed me on the street and turned around to try to get me in the car with them. They asked me if I was lost and told me to get in the car with them. I said no, but they continued to try. I continued to say no, and then I took off running home and told my mother.

Washington was where I first experienced hatred and discrimination from a teacher. My first grade teacher was Mrs. Lawson, and she was a great lady and teacher. My second grade teacher was Mr. Watson, and he was just the opposite. He would make me sit in the back of the classroom and would very seldom help me, if at all. One day while in class, I needed to use the bathroom to go urinate urgently. I was in dire straits and was losing my grip on holding my urine. I raised my hand repeatedly, but Mr. Watson ignored me. I was very restless and quite fidgety in my seat because I was getting so close to urinating on myself. Suddenly, Mr. Watson walked very fast and sternly to the back of the room. I thought he was coming to ask me what I wanted, but instead he just grabbed me by the arm and walked me outside. He planted me just outside the portable classroom in the frigid, cold weather and told me to stand and stay. He never asked me what I wanted. Good thing I had my coat, which I had put on to cover the fact that I needed to go to the bathroom badly. Right before Mr. Watson went back into the classroom, I told him I needed to pee oh so badly, but once again, he ignored me before going back in and shutting the door. Well, I couldn't hold my urine anymore, so I took off running to the bathroom that was located twenty yards away in the school building. Remember, my classroom was portable. I made it to the bathroom stall just in time and began to urinate in the toilet when suddenly, the stall door swung and slammed open and scared me nearly to death. It was Mr. Watson who forced the door open. He just picked me up while I was still urinating and carried me back to the spot outside the portable room where I was before and set me down and told me not to move. I was not able to zip my pants up, but I attempted as Mr. Watson carried me back to the portable room. He stood me in that spot again with my pants soaked with urine. My mother was called, and she came and picked me up. I am not sure what happened when my mom and Mr. Watson talked, but I am sure I was made out to be in the wrong. To this day, I never thought about the fact that the entire class must have been watching the whole ordeal from the window. For second graders, I am most sure the whole thing seemed funny, but it was an unfunny thing to me. I was probably not the only kid that Mr. Watson targeted and mistreated, but I sure hope he got what he deserved, which was to not be a teacher.

We lived in Tacoma/Fort Lewis for a few years until 1969, and one day, Dad received orders to go to Vietnam. With Dad receiving orders to go to Vietnam and with Mom far along in her pregnancy with Velvet, Mom refused to move back to Texas, where family and help were. Mom convinced Dad to have us stay on the West Coast, so Dad moved us to live with some of his family in Los Angeles, California. And that family was Dad's cousin, Oliver Dirks, and his wife and kids. Living in Los Angeles was so expensive, so Dad found us an apartment in San Fernando Valley, California, and in June 1969, that's where we moved to.

CHAPTER FOUR

Dad receives orders to go Vietnam, and he leaves us behind in San Fernando Valley, California, from June 1969 to June 1970; we have direct encounters with the Black Panther Party; I get in the middle of an altercation with a famous black female activist

T
he time was June 1969. Dad moved the family to some large apartment complex in San Fernando Valley, California, right before he was to leave for Vietnam. Dad had to complete a tour of duty in Vietnam as part of his army requirement. While we lived in San Fernando Valley, Mom's behavior was quite good and stable because she knew she needed to be strong while Dad was gone. During that one year, Mom had no mental issues, but the family would face some challenges that probably affected Mom's mental stability later. I would say that Dad kept Mom's mental illness from us kids very well, and I thank him for that. I believe during our stay in San Fernando Valley, Mom was at her strongest and bravest.

There were a few incidents we faced that brought us close as a family. One night, we witnessed the Black Panther Party flex their muscles. We watched them attempt to unlawfully enter an apartment with a family still inside, and that apartment was about seventy-five yards away from us. About twenty members walked up a set of stairs to the apartment and demanded that the occupants open the door and exit. Apparently, the occupants refused, so the BP members threw trash cans at the front door and tried to break the door down. Their efforts did not work, and the twenty-member gang left the area, probably because the occupants were totally barricaded inside, or they threatened to shoot through the door, or they threatened to call the police, or maybe the Black Panther Party was just using a scare tactic. Either way, they never broke the door down nor entered the apartment. On a separate night, about a dozen of the Black Panther Party attempted another unlawful entry into an apartment that was directly underneath ours. As we watched the victimization of the apartment below us, which was very terrifying, we couldn't stop thinking that they would come to our upstairs apartment next because we were watching them. We watched the group throw large boulders through the window and break the door down. I am not sure if anyone was at home at the time. When we looked at the apartment the next morning, it was completely empty and trashed, and it looked like it was beyond repair. It was as if the people knew the Black Panthers were coming for them and had left prior to them coming.

Another serious incident would occur that involved us directly—and far too closely, I might add. I believe the day was a Saturday because we were not in school that morning. When we woke up that Saturday morning, Mom noticed that another car had parked really close to ours. Dad had purchased a tan or beige two-door 1966 Buick Skylark, and he was extremely proud of that car. Well, Mom went on about her business getting us prepared for the day. I believe she had an appointment with the doctor because she was pregnant with Velvet. Mom was probably seven, maybe eight, months pregnant. Velvet would be born on October 28, 1969. Well, Mom could look out of the back window of our apartment, which was upstairs, and could see our car very well. Our car was parked hood-first up against a four-foot cement wall. Later, as Mom looked at our car, she noticed that the hood was up. There was a car parked very close to ours, and its hood was up as well. Things looked suspicious to Mom because she saw the owner of the other car tinkering around underneath the hood of ours. Mom immediately got one of her male friends who lived across from us, and by the time they walked out to the cars, the hood of both cars were down. Mom got in our car to start it, maybe to move it, but the engine would not turn over. There was absolutely no sign of life in the vehicle. Mom's friend lifted the hood up and noticed that the battery was not in our car. Mom's friend confronted the man who had parked really close to our car and discovered that he had taken our car battery and placed it in his car. Mom's friend made the thief put our car battery back. The thief didn't even live in those apartments, but he was forced to leave, and the police were not called. An incident like that never occurred again.

Another incident happened to our family that was really life-threatening. One day, Mom gathered us all up and had us get into the car, and we drove to visit one of Mom's good male friends named Sam. He was an older man, probably some twenty to thirty years older than Mom. We used to call him Uncle Sam. We spent a lot of time at Uncle Sam's house. He had a beautiful garden, and we spent a lot of time in it, either cleaning it or planting seeds or pulling produce out to eat. He grew lots of vegetables, and one of my least favorable vegetables that Uncle Sam was extremely fond of was orange squash. The way he prepared that squash was so tasty that I thought it was a pumpkin dish, only to find out later that squash is in the pumpkin family.

We spent the whole day at his house, but it soon came time to leave, so we left Uncle Sam's house for the evening before it got dark. Mom was driving home through a small part of town. As Mom drove west, we had to stop at a four-way traffic light intersection. Our car was first in line at the red light, and the light turned green for the other vehicles in traffic to go. Suddenly, coming from our left side heading north, a white Volkswagen bug going at an above-normal speed drove right in front of us and into the parking lot of a convenience store located to our right. It came to a complete stop in the parking lot. Suddenly, the driver got out of the Volkswagen bug with some type of rifle and began shooting this man who was crossing the street just a few feet in front of us. Several bullets hit the man, and he fell to the ground in the middle of the crosswalk, and to our complete shock and surprise, one of those bullets hit our car. We heard it as it hit our car. Mom was terrified and knew our car was hit, so she immediately put the car in reverse and turned around and went right back to Uncle Sam's house. Mom was hysterical and frantic as she ran to get Uncle Sam. We all got out of the car and saw a bullet hole in the front right side quarter panel of the car. We were all blessed that day because none of us were hit or hurt, and our car didn't sustain any major damage as far as I could remember. It was still drivable. Sometime later, we were told that the shooting was an ordered hit by the Black Panther Party.

And yes, we would have yet another incident happening in our family. It was some time after Velvet was born, which was October 28, 1969. I would say Velvet was probably about four months old, a good recommended age to take a baby outside after it was born. Since Dad was in Vietnam and he knew Mom and us five kids would need some help, he got the army to set up a midwife to take care of us while Mom recuperated from having Velvet. The midwife was a white lady, probably in her sixties, and her name was Agnes Goods. She was the greatest and nicest lady anyone could ever meet. Well, I believe this next incident was close to February 16 because Mom was taking me to get a haircut for my birthday. I was the only one who got a haircut that day. Me, Mom, my brothers Wayne and Ross, and my sisters Farrah and Velvet—who was just a baby in the stroller—went into a familiar barbershop. Mom knew the owner of the barbershop. Mom got the attention of a lady barber and gave her instructions on how she wanted her to cut my hair. Mom and my siblings left the barbershop for just a few moments and came back. I don't believe the lady barber was even finished with my hair, but Mom did not like what she saw. Mom and the lady barber got into a shouting altercation, and Mom quickly pulled me out of the barber's chair. Mom and the lady barber continued to exchange hostile words with each other, and then suddenly, the lady barber grabbed a pair of scissors as to maybe try to harm my mother. Mom reacted to defend herself, reaching into her purse and pulling out a large barbecue fork. All this while I was in between them. Mom grabbed all of us, backed us out of the barbershop, and we left. Mom immediately drove to a friend's house that was close to the barbershop to talk about the incident. Shortly afterward, we got back into the car and started driving home, and then we noticed the lady barber walking away from the barbershop with her bags and other items. Mom went back to the barbershop a few weeks later, and the owner of the barbershop told Mom he had fired the lady barber because she had behaved like that with other customers before and he ran out of patience with her. The owner of the barbershop also told Mom that the lady barber was a female activist and was involved off and on with the Black Panther Party. Later, we would find out that she would progress to being a big voice and a prominent figure as a black activist in the 1970s, assisting the black equality movement for many years.

Living in San Fernando Valley was rough most of the time. I learned that people were mean and hateful. I also learned not to steal after a certain incident I was involved in. My best friend Newton and I went to a convenience store to buy ice cream. Well, we saw some large red popsicles we wanted, but they were too expensive for us to buy, so Newton decided that we would steal them, but I was not in agreement with that idea. Newton talked about how we could get out of the store without paying. We walked around with the popsicles in hand for a few seconds, and without warning, Newton ran out of the store with his popsicle. Well, the store manager must have been watching us because he quickly ran after Newton. Another store clerk grabbed me and told me that if Newton was not caught, they would call the police, and we would go to jail. Newton was caught shortly afterward, and the store manager told us both that they would not call the police but that we could never come back to their store again. A few weeks later, I did go back to the convenience store, but I wore a full face mask like the one worn by Spiderman but white. They never knew who I was, and I never went back to that store. I just wanted to see if I could get away with not being noticed.

One day, I was walking home by myself from Newton's house, and my house was about four or five blocks away. Well, I came to walk past these three white teenagers who were about seventeen years old. They were standing up against a four-foot brick wall next to the main street. Once I walked past them, I turned to look at them, and then they started running after me. I was a fast runner back then, so I ran across the busy intersection and into an office building. I went into an elevator and went up two floors. I pretended like I exited off that floor but stayed hidden in the elevator. The three white teenagers couldn't find me and were on a floor somewhere looking for me. I went back down in the elevator to the first floor and ran out all the way home. I never saw those teenagers again.

About a week later, Wayne and I were at the playground located in the middle section of our apartment complex when all of a sudden, some kids started shooting us with a slingshot. Wayne, who was not afraid to fight, confronted one of the kids and started fighting. Wayne kicked that kid's ass, and for some strange reason, the other kid came over to fight me, but all I was doing was playing in the sandbox with my small toys. I was not a fighter, and both of my pockets were filled with small toys. We began to fight—or let me say that the other kid was fighting me because I didn't know how to fight at that time, and he was kicking my ass. Since Wayne had beat up his kid, he then came over and beat up the kid that was kicking my ass. Wayne grabbed me by the arm, and we ran home. Wayne and I also had a friend named Corbin, and he was probably our best friend in the apartments, but he was cruel to animals. One day, Corbin cornered a cat inside a playground obstacle and began throwing rocks at it until he killed it. I never liked that but wasn't strong enough to tell Corbin that was wrong and to stop. June 1970 came around, and it was time for us to move from San Fernando Valley, California. Dad's next duty station would be Fort Conquest, Louisiana.

CHAPTER FIVE

Dad is stationed at Fort Conquest and we live in
New Contact, Louisiana; Mom's mental illness comes
in full bloom and really shows its ugly beauty; we
experience a third burning of epic proportions

I t is June 1970, and Dad returned from Vietnam. We were ordered
to move from that godforsaken San Fernando Valley, and it
couldn't have come any sooner for me. We were moving to Dad's
new duty station of Fort Conquest, Louisiana. The household items
were loaded and packed away on a Mayflower moving van. Dad loaded
us up in his Buick Skylark sedan, and we began our drive out of San
Fernando Valley and said good riddance to that horrible place. Dad
did not tell us where we were going, only that we were moving to be
closer to family. The long drive across three states for a total of over
1800 miles was fun at first, stopping and playing at rest areas, but the
long drive quickly became nerve-racking with five kids and two parents
in one car towing a small U-Haul trailer. After such a long drive over
the course of a few days, we finally made it to the state of Texas, and as
we got closer to familiar country, you could see the excitement on our
parents' faces—especially Dad, and not so much on Mom's face. We
first stopped in Dolphin and met Mom's side of the family, and then
were on to West Daytona to meet Dad's side of the family. It was very
fun meeting and realizing that I had family like cousins and uncles and

aunts. We did not stay overnight, and we continued our travels to the city of Leesville, Louisiana.

We would live in a small town just minutes on the outskirts of Leesville called New Contact. Dad already had a house for us at 727 Elm Street. When we arrived at the house that dark evening in June 1970, I thought the house was perfect. It was a three-bedroom, two-bathroom house with a beautiful front and backyard from what I could see that night. There were crickets hopping all around the street in front of our new house, probably because there was a streetlight directly out front. There were frogs jumping and leaping around as well. It was really cool for me because I loved animals of all kinds. I was so excited. New Contact would be a place we would live in the longest—six years. By the time we moved from there in June 1976, I would be happy and sad at the same time. Still, it was a great place to live because it was the place where I met my first girlfriend, Cassie Dawn Styles, who I truly loved. And I also had my second best true friend in the whole wide world, Robert Bill Dallas. Bill was a black male around the same age as me, and we had so much in common that we were inseparable. I also had some great white friends who lived across the street named Wayne, Gary, and Johnny Sullivan. New Contact would also be the place where I would see the timeless classic films *The Exorcist*, *Richard Pryor: Live in Concert*, and the unforgettable first installment of *Friday the 13th*—which became a cult classic and was legendary in my own sight. I would also have my best track season, anchoring my eighth grade 440-yard relay and mile-relay track team to first place finishes. I would also see my dad kiss my mom for the first and only time in my life. That kiss was memorable, charming, and securing. Our family would also survive a category two tornado, which hopped right over our house one scary night and would destroy a house behind us two streets over. Dad would also leave our mother and go live with another woman a few years later, but the most horrific thing to happen there was that Mom's mental illness would reveal itself to the entire family in full form.

There would be several incidents involving Mom's mental illness while living in New Contact. One of the first incidents I remember is one night, there was a scary lightning storm. The thunder and lightning

28

was quite terrifying that evening, and Mom requested that the entire family get into her and Dad's bed. I don't think Dad agreed with that idea, but he went along with it anyway. He went along with it as if he knew something more was coming. It was like he had experienced some bad behavior from Mom before and knew how to handle the situation. I guess Mom was just afraid for us kids and wanted all of us in the room together safe, and we stayed really quiet and didn't move. The storm would eventually move on to the next county, and we went on with our activities.

Another incident that would take place and show Mom was becoming more unstable was when she loaded us all in the car and drove to the city of Leesville to do some shopping at the Benjamin Franklin store. We got to the Benjamin Franklin store, and Mom drove around looking for a parking spot but couldn't find one. After driving around for a couple of minutes, she found one spot and was about to pull into it when suddenly, a white man quickly cut in front of our car and parked into the spot. Mom was furious and tried talking to the man, but he wouldn't listen and continued to walk into the store. Mom drove off and found another spot and parked the car. Mom waited for the man to go completely into the store, and then she reached into the glove compartment and grabbed a red Chinese letter opener, got out of the car, sneaked over to the man's car, and kneeled down to stabs the tires. Mom quickly walked back to the car, and we drove away. When Mom arrived at our house, she surprisingly drove on the grass and parked the tan 1966 Buick Skylark in the backyard. For some forty years, I was not sure if anything happened after that—like if the police were called, or if the man knew that it was Mom who flattened his tires,—but I finally conversed with Dad, and he told me that the police sought him out for Mom's vandalism. Dad was ordered to pay $600 to replace the man's tires. Dad said that was a real blow at that time simply because $600 back in 1976 is equivalent to $2512 in 2016. Dad had to pay it, or it would have been a big strike against him, since he was in the army.

Another incident that took place was when we were preparing to go visit family in West Daytona and Dolphin. Dad's family lived in West Daytona, and Mom's family lived in Dolphin. The two cities were eight miles apart. The trip would take approximately under four hours. As we were preparing to leave, packing up clothes and food and shutting the house down, Mom started acting unlike her pleasant and loving self. She was acting irrational, compulsive, scattered, unsure of herself, and unclear of her decisions. She would go do something and then undo the same thing. Dad would kindly ask her to calm down and relax, and she would, but it was short lived. At a point, Dad spoke to Mom and said, "Delores, you have been awake for several days now, and you need to get some rest." I remember Mom had been awake for four or five days straight. I can't imagine her state of mind, much less her physical state. I get irritated, antsy, and nervous if I don't get sleep after I have been up all day. I am not sure if Mom was awake completely the whole four or five days or if she would take naps periodically, but either way she had been awake for quite a long time. Mom's behavior would continue to get odd and strange. My brothers and sisters seemed to be unfazed by her behavior, or maybe they just didn't notice, but I know I did. Dad tried to get Mom to lay down and get some sleep before we traveled, and Mom made several attempts to sleep, but her efforts were unsuccessful. Mom would constantly get up and out of her bed and go from room to room asking if we were all right. After a while, Mom would lay down and sleep for an hour or more—at least we thought she slept, but in actuality she didn't sleep at all. By then I think the time was around 2:00 or 3:00 a.m., and Dad must have felt like Mom was fine, so we all loaded into the car and drove away to go visit family.

But as I am writing this and getting more details from Dad, he says his plan was not to travel to go visit family but to take Mom to the hospital in Fort Conquest, and he did a great job of disguising what he was trying to do. Dad pulled out of the driveway, accelerated, and turned left going up Hickory Street. We came to the first stop sign about two hundred yards away. He kept straight for about another two hundred yards and stopped at the next stop sign. Dad turned left and drove about a hundred yards to the next stop sign that was located at the entrance to our neighborhood. What happened next blew everyone's mind. Dad accelerated to turn left onto another street that would lead us to a main street. As I sat directly behind Mom in the car and got comfortable enough to start to fall asleep because it was two or three in the morning, suddenly, without any warning, Mom opened the car door. Yeah, Mom opened the door while the car was moving. Dad must have been driving at about thirty miles per hour. The opening of the door startled me, but I was not afraid because I just thought Mom was throwing something out of the door. But it was a little bit scary looking at the door and seeing the street move in the darkness as the car's interior lights shined upon it. Normally you would roll down the window to throw something out if you really needed, but I never saw Mom throw anything out. Suddenly, I heard Dad with a calm but stern voice telling Mom to close the door, and Mom did close the door without any further incident. Dad drove about another fifty yards or so, and Mom opened the door again, and once again, Dad told her to close the door with a little more command. When Mom refused, Dad raised his hand and hit Mom on the shoulder, hoping it would make her straighten up and stop doing that. Mom did close the door, and Dad continued to drive down that stretch of road for about a mile, and then we came on to the main road of a major intersection.

At that intersection was mine and Wayne's favorite convenience store called Adolph's, and it was to our left. We used to love to go to that store and buy candy and soda pop, especially the candy called Now and Later with its assorted flavors. Chocolate and banana was my favorite. Anyway, Dad then put on his turn signal to turn right, and we turned right. Even in the early hours of the morning, I was a little bit confused because normally we would turn left at that intersection to travel to go see family. I remembered because we had made that turn at least a half dozen times before. I did question and say to myself, *Maybe Dad has a new direction that he hasn't shared with us.* But I still thought it was strange and out of the usual that Dad turned right. For more than forty years, I would often replay that incident in my mind. That right turn bothered me for many years and left me questioning every time I would think of that strange life-changing moment in the car. You see, for at least the first few years that we lived in New Contact, and with the many times we traveled to visit our families in West Daytona and Dolphin, we always turned left at that intersection. Now as I write this book some forty-plus years after that puzzling right turn, I think I now know why Dad turned right that night. I have never talked to Dad about that strange morning car ride, but I now believe I know why he turned right—he was attempting to take Mom to the army hospital located in Fort Conquest.

As a matter of fact, it just occurred to me now as I write this book that Dad had been planning to go to the hospital for a few days, but he just didn't know how to go about it, so I believe he devised a plan of packing up everybody's clothes and food only as a decoy. We were never going to travel to see family that night. And again as I write this memoir, I recall that at some point earlier in the evening of that strange night, Dad had said that "Mom has not been to sleep for a few days." Can anyone imagine not sleeping for one day, much more three or four days! Mom must have been in a serious state of confusion and pain. There was absolutely no way Dad would jeopardize our lives and well-being by taking a four-hour trip in the condition that Mom was in. Back then, Dad was a very private and respected man, and because of the fact that he was a top drill sergeant in the army and had a lot of men under his command, he probably didn't want any of our neighbors knowing that Mom was in the type of condition that she was in. He probably didn't want an ambulance pulling up to our house, alerting our neighbors no matter what time of the day it was. You know how neighbors are, they would have tried to pry into our business.

My suspicions were correct because I spoke to Dad about those eventful and terrifying few days, and I got clear and concise details about that night. He confirmed what I was thinking. After Dad turned right at that intersection where Adolph's was, he drove on down the street, picking up speed to about fifty miles per hour, and traveled about a mile. Suddenly, it happened again. Mom opened the door once again, and now I was starting to get scared. I remember Dad's words very clear, and he said very sternly and a little loudly, "Amanda, close the door." Mom closed the door. Dad continued to drive down the road for a few feet and suddenly, Mom opened the door again. I can't remember exactly what Mom said, but I believe she said, "Bruce Shelton, I know what you are trying to do, you are trying to take me to the hospital, and there is nothing wrong with me." Mom may not have been in a good state of mind that night, but I believe she knew that Dad was trying to take her to the hospital, and that was why she opened the door. By now, Dad was extremely upset, and while still driving, he quickly reached across Mom's lap and grabbed the car door handle and pulled it shut while sternly saying, "Close the door. We are going back home." He made a very quick U-turn, and we headed home. As I sat behind Mom in the car, I was feeling her pain, and it made me sad seeing and hearing her that way. I did not know what to do, but I suddenly thought of two things: one was to pray for her, and the other was a wish of mine. I wished that Mom's illness or sickness could go into me so that she wouldn't have the problem anymore and would be all right. I wished that right from my seat behind Mom. Obviously, it didn't work, but that was how much I wanted to help my mother.

We inevitably made it back home without any more incidents. We all went back into the house and into our rooms to go back to sleep. A few moments passed by, and then I heard Dad speaking to Mom with his voice raised a little bit. Dad was telling her that she needed to lay down and go to sleep. Suddenly, Mom called for all of us kids to come to her room, and we all went to her room and lay on the bed. We tried to go to sleep, but Mom kept getting up and checking on something, and I had no idea what it was. Mom would come back to lay down but once again get up. Suddenly, Mom wanted us all to go to the living room, so we all did and sat down on the couch. The entire time, Mom would ask us kids if we were all right. By now we were extremely tired and really wanted to just go to sleep, but now Mom wanted us to go back to her bedroom. We went and got on the bed. Dad was relatively calm, but again told her that she needed to go to sleep. Suddenly, Mom pulled a barbecue pitchfork on Dad. Apparently, the fork was under her pillow. Dad didn't appear to be afraid or startled but did hold up a pillow to fend off the small jabs that Mom was poking at him. He told her to stop. Mom jabbed the fork at him again, but it didn't appear to me that she wanted to hurt or harm him. Nonetheless, she was jabbing at him. During this incident, Dad was laughing and acting as if the entire incident was funny. As I look back and replay that incident in my mind, I now know that was Dad's way of dealing with Mom's condition and unpredictable and irrational behavior. He behaved that way to keep the situation at a calm and manageable level so as not to scare or alarm us kids. Dad was a big 6'2" muscle-strapped man who weighed about 250 pounds, and he could have no doubt manhandled Mom, but because of his upbringing and love for his own mother, he didn't. The technique worked at least for me—I was never afraid of Mom's behavior because Dad seemed to not be afraid, and I did look up to my dad and respected him a lot. Now I know what Mom was doing when she was getting up and in and out of the bed—she wanted to retrieve the fork without Dad's knowledge. But all the while Dad remained alert.

Things stayed relatively calm for a little while that night until I saw some flashing red lights through the living room window. Dad got out of the bed, went to the front room, and opened the front door. It was the sheriff, and an ambulance parked backward in the driveway. At some point, Dad called for help, but the hospital staff probably told him to make every attempt to bring her in first, and his efforts fell short. I remember there was a struggle to get Mom to go with the health care workers and get her into the ambulance, and soon the sheriff entered our house and tried to assist. But Mom was slightly combative and physical with the sheriff, so he ended up refraining from forcing her. The sheriff used his training to talk to her and eventually convinced her to go with the military health care workers, and she got into the ambulance of her own free will. All of us watched her walk out the door and into the ambulance. It was such a sad scene for us. I don't remember Mom kissing us goodbye but I do remember that the workers were surrounding her to keep us safe as they walked her to the ambulance. I remember that she was standing up with her head outside the ambulance window, yelling to us and saying she loved us. Dad loaded all of us into the car, and we drove behind the ambulance as it drove onward to the hospital in Fort Conquest. We made it to the hospital, and Dad parked the car. He went in with Mom and the health care workers and left us in the car. To me, it seemed like hours passed. As far as I know it could have been only minutes, but it seemed like hours. Suddenly, I saw Dad walking toward us. He got into the car, and I asked him how Mom was doing.

He replied that she had a nervous breakdown. He also said that they had to give her shock treatment because she was fighting the nurses. They first attempted to give her a shot to calm her down, but the needle broke in her arm. They then had to hold and strap her down to give her shock treatment, and it worked. He said that she was resting and that she would be fine and we would see her later. That was the first time I would hear the words *nervous breakdown* and *shock treatment*. Now, I had absolutely no idea what that meant, and I didn't even bother to ask Dad, but he said it with comfort and assurance that it would help Mom, and that was good enough for me.

I must share with those who may not know and understand what shock treatment is. One day, I watched a movie that would give me a complete understanding of shock treatment. The movie gave me an inside look of what it was and exactly what my mother went through when she received it. I finally watched the movie *One Flew Over the Cuckoo's Nest* starring Jack Nicholson, and when I say finally, I mean some twenty years after its release. I didn't watch that movie when it first came out in 1975 because I had absolutely no interest in seeing it simply because of its name. The name made it seem like some dumb movie about birds, and a musical at that. How wrong I was. I heard so much stuff about that movie that I got sick of hearing about it. Even with its awards, I just couldn't bring myself to watch it. But one day in 1995, I would watch it, and it would change my life forever and show me what my mother went through when she received shock treatment at the state hospital. There is a scene in it that showed how shock treatment was administered, and when I saw that procedure, I cried and sobbed for minutes for my mother. What cruelty and pain she went through. I am surprised she didn't have a lot of brain damage from that procedure. It seemed inhuman, and it just made me love my mother that much more. And by the way, *One Flew Over the Cuckoo's Nest* is without a doubt an excellent film, opening the doors to mental health hospitals and its patients. If you haven't seen the movie, I highly recommend you do.

Now let me continue. We drove home and went straight to bed after that trip to the hospital in Fort Conquest. Two weeks passed by, and Dad eventually told us kids that Mom had to be transferred to the state hospital, a mental health facility in Pineville, Louisiana. As time passed, we would constantly ask Dad where Mom was and when was she coming home. Dad finally had some answers for us after we asked him a hundred times, and he said that Mom was in a mental health hospital in Pineville and that it was far away. He went on to tell us that he had planned several trips for us all to go visit her, and we were ecstatic to learn of this wonderful news. We were going to see our mother.

One weekend, Dad packed a very big lunch for us to take on our visit to Mom because he had received word that she was well enough for us to see her. Dad fried a lot of chicken for all of us and made some potato salad and brought bread and something to drink. It smelled so damn good in the car on the way that I couldn't contain myself. Traveling to Pineville almost seemed like a regular weekend trip for us because we went so often. Dad was a good father and husband doing that for such a long time, and he managed well to take care of us and maintain his superiority as a decorated drill sergeant. Dad would drive a two-hour round-trip to visit Mom in Pineville. I remember the first time we went to visit her and how the drive there was unlike any other we had gone on mainly because Mom was not sitting in the car with us. I felt numb the entire trip because I didn't know what to expect as a fourteen-year-old. My mother was not right, and it bothered me, but it didn't make me think that she would die. We finally made it to the state hospital, and we had to drive into a guarded and gated facility. I had not seen anything like it in my young life. We all were so anxious to see Mom. Dad parked and went into the main office while we remained in the car. After about fifteen minutes, Dad came out, made it back to the car, and then drove to another building. Once we got to the other building, we got out of the car, and Dad grabbed the basket of food he had prepared. We all walked over to a bench located outside and sat down. The bench was in a very nice area that had lots of trees. There were a few birdbaths around, and there was beautiful sunshine. There were quite a few squirrels running around too.

It seemed like forever before Mom came out, but finally she did. Mom was dressed in white pants with a white button-up top, a light blue T-shirt, and white stretch shoes. Mom walked toward us a little slowly. When I first saw her up close, she had a look on her face like she was embarrassed, but I didn't care because I was so happy to see her. She hugged us all and told us she loved us. We sat around and ate the food that Dad had brought, and we talked and just had a good time. Mom appeared to be tired and still a little bit confused. Then I heard her and Dad talking, and I heard her ask him, "When will I be able to go home, Bruce Shelton?" Dad replied, "Once you get better, Mandy." Dad used to call her Mandy because it was short for Amanda. Now about an hour passed, and our visit was over and it was time to go. Visits at first were short because of the patient's condition. Mom kissed and hugged us all, and she walked back with an escort into her living facility. Mom showed little emotion because she was under medication. We all cried, as it was really painful not having her ride back home with us. We would get back home, and we wouldn't know what to do. As for me, I would sit at home a lot wondering what Mom was doing and how she was feeling. As I look back on our family and how we dealt with Mom's condition as kids, I note that we never received counseling. I don't know if counseling was available for kids, or if Dad was not aware that we were affected by it, or if even Mom thought that we were affected by it. I can say she was not concerned about us receiving counseling because she didn't receive any when she was a kid as far as I know. I never had thoughts to ask anybody who may have known, and the most important people who may have known have passed away now. The military health care providers may have offered it to us, and Dad maybe turned it down because we appeared to be normal, but we were anything but normal. We would visit Mom a few more times at the state hospital in Pineville before she would come home. Mom would have several more relapses in her mental illness in the six years we would live in New Contact, and just like the other times, she would have to go back to Pineville. There were times when relatives on Mom's side of the family like Thomas James Timpson and Big Pa, Peter Deal Sr., would come and stay with us to help Dad out. Thomas James would come so often that he had a girlfriend in Leesville. Thomas James was such a good man and was funny to be around.

Let me speak about my dad a little bit. Dad for the most part is a very quiet man. As far as I remember, Dad didn't go out with the guys and drink and party and be out late in the night. Dad would come home after work and go to his room. Dad had a lawn chair set up in the bedroom, and he would prop up his feet and occasionally drink a beer. Dad never got drunk. Dad would smoke his cigarettes, and his favorite brand back then was Winston. He loved that cigarette brand until he quit smoking some twenty-plus years later. Dad would help Mom prepare food a lot and would play basketball with me and Wayne often in the backyard. Dad and I used to race each other down Elm Street, and he would throw a football and softball with me in front of the house. The one thing I enjoyed the most with Dad was going fishing and boy, how I loved fishing, as you know from an earlier chapter. Dad would take me and Wayne fishing at Toledo Bend Dam a lot. Toledo Bend Dam was located right between the border state line of Texas and Louisiana, and boy, it was a great fishing spot. Dad and I would catch most of the fish, and Wayne wouldn't because he lacked the patience to fish, and sometimes he didn't catch any at all. We would bring home lots of largemouth bass, and we would scale the fish, clean them, and give them to the best fry cook in the world, our mother. We would have some good times eating fresh fried largemouth bass. Wayne and I would catch crayfish quite often, spending hours fishing and bringing home pots of crayfish. My mom would boil them for us, and we would have a blast eating them.

Quickly, the tune of the house would change, as Mom appeared stable and normal. We had our mother back, and she was operating on all thrusters. For some strange reason, Farrah was getting into trouble a lot. She was getting whippings more times than I care to remember. Farrah was getting whippings so often that Mom would ask Wayne and me to catch her and hold her down because she would escape Mom's clutches and run away all over the house. She had gotten really good at running away from Mom. She would make her way to the bathroom and lock herself inside for long periods of time. It appeared to me that Mom was not able to open the door, and Farrah was not opening it. That tactic made Mom so mad that she didn't know what to do. Like

I said, Mom would speak to Wayne and me and ask us to catch Farrah so that she could whip her, and so we did. Wayne and I would corner Farrah in her room, and Mom would come and tell us to hold her down before whipping the living daylights out of her. Most of the time I thought it was funny. I never thought it was wrong because I felt like Farrah deserved it. Farrah would steal Mom's stuff like jewelry, and she would cut her own hair with scissors and would just misbehave. Now, as I look back on those whippings, I am not sure if Farrah really deserved all of them. I think Mom was just mad at Farrah and harbored negative feelings for her, maybe because she got burned when she was two years old, or maybe because Mom was still furious from when Farrah pulled down her underwear for Wayne to see her private parts.

At some point when I was around thirty-five years old, I asked Mom why she whipped Farrah so much. I asked that question while Mom and I were laughing and talking about incidents that had happened over the years. One story that Mom told me really stuck out for me, and Mom said that Farrah would act naughty when she was in the presence of Dad. I don't believe Dad did anything inappropriate, and I don't believe Farrah was being naughty with Dad. I believe Dad was trying to have a good and pure relationship with his daughter, and Farrah adored her dad like most girls do. Maybe Mom was threatened by the attention Dad used to give Farrah and was jealous. But what I believe is that Mom remembered how Big Pa used to interact with her, and it may have been inappropriate by the way Nana explained it. One day I was talking to Mom, and she brought up that Nana didn't like her at times because of the relationship she and Big Pa had. Mom told me that she really liked the relationship she and Big Pa had, and that it was kind and very loving and she felt protected by him. Kids feeling protected is a great, stable trait, which allows kids to grow healthy. Mom also told me Nana had said to her that she thought Big Pa was inappropriate with her, and that statement really hurt Mom because she was very fond of Big Pa. And Big Pa really cared for her, which explains why he came to help Dad out with Mom as often as he could over the years. However, Mom disciplined Farrah a lot, and their relationship would get worse over the years.

Months and days passed by, and it was time for us to go visit family again in Dolphin and West Daytona, so the car was loaded up, and we took off like we normally did. When Dad got to that one familiar intersection which was adjacent to Adolph's, Dad did take a left turn, and I was relieved. We traveled for nearly four hours, some 230 miles, and we made it to Dad's parents' house. We visited for a little and then headed to Dolphin to visit Mom's family. We were about two miles from Nana's house when Dad suddenly pulled the car over onto the side of the road, and Dad and Mom argued. They argued for about five minutes, and what they were arguing about I don't remember. We had never seen them argue before, and it was quite strange, disturbing, and unsettling. I realized later that Mom was having a relapse in her mental illness, a nervous breakdown. We made it to Nana's house and visited for a while, but Mom and Dad did not stay long. They left me, Wayne, and Ross at Nana's house so that we could play, learn, and bond with our cousin Pete, whose real name was Peter Deal Jr. Pete was Nana and Big Pa's only son, and he was like the greatest big brother that anybody could ever have. Usually when we stayed, we would stay for several weeks, but this time we would stay longer. Farrah and Velvet stayed at Dad's parents' house so they could play, learn, and bond with our aunties, who were Dad's sisters Angie Rock, Betty Ann Rock, and our grandmother, Catherine Rock, or Cattie. It seemed like a planned-out visit, as Mom and Dad went back home to Leesville. Wayne was around sixteen years old, Ross was around eight years old, and I was around fourteen years old. Wayne and I had so much fun being with Pete; it was incredible. He took us fishing, hunting, and crabbing, and he took us to his job, which was so much fun. His job was just right up the street at a plant store. We used to help him water plants and tend to the plants throughout the facility. The owner was Mrs. Twiggs, who lived right across the street. She was a great lady too.

It's the week of the Fourth of July, and Pete had taken us to get some fireworks. One night, Pete chased me and Wayne down the street while firing a Roman candle at us. I would have to say that fireballs whizzing by our heads was dangerous, yet so fun and exciting. I had no doubt that Pete had no intentions of hitting us, or maybe he did! A few days later, we would see a traumatic and unforgettable incident that would change our lives forever. That day had come, and the evening was winding down. It was getting late, and like clockwork, we were preparing our baths like we usually did—by boiling water in a large pot. Because the house did not have a boiler or a hot water heater, we would boil water on top of the stove and use the boiled water carefully for two reasons. The first reason was to pour the boiling hot water over the freshly washed dishes to sterilize them, and the other reason was to use it to take baths. Once the water had come to a boil, we would grab the large pot of water and walk it to the bathtub to pour it in. We then would add cold water to make it warm to wash ourselves. I am not sure whose time it was to take a bath that night, but the pot of boiled water on the stove was ready. Now, at the same time, Pete's sister, Layla, who was around sixteen years old, was sweeping the floor and standing right side of the stove, just two feet away. The pot of boiling water was on the right rear burner on the stove. I was standing in the kitchen on the right side of the stove about six feet away, and my brother Ross, who was also in the kitchen on his knees to my right, was almost in front of the stove yet four feet away. Wayne was sitting at the kitchen table to my far right, behind Ross. With Layla's back toward the boiling pot of water, she continued to sweep the kitchen floor, and then she and Ross began to play with each other with the broom, and Ross innocently grabbed the straw broom to play with her as well. Layla must have sensed the danger that the pot of boiling water would have caused if it had rocked and spilled, so she used the broom to push Ross away, but he may have thought she was still playing and decided to grab her leg at the ankle. Suddenly, he pulled her leg hard toward him, and Layla began to lose her balance and started falling. As she began to fall, she reached behind herself without looking and grabbed the edge of the pot of boiling water. Layla fell to the ground on her stomach while bringing the pot of boiling water down on her back. What an eerie coincidence that Ross would be involved in another burning incident almost ten years from when a pot of boiling water dropped on our mother's foot just moments after she put Ross out of the way. Once again, Ross did not get burned at all because he managed somehow to get out of the way. Layla belted out this bloodcurdling scream at the top of her lungs and quickly jumped and ran forward to the adjacent bedroom. Because the scream was so horrific, Pete heard her and ran out of his room that was connected to the room that Layla ran into. He saw her jumping up and down and swirling all around and saw her shirt steaming like smoke. Pete reacted without hesitation and grabbed his sister, pulling that shirt clean off her body. I was most sure Pete burned his fingers when he took that shirt off, as the white blouse was still steaming after it hit the floor. Pete then pulled a sheet off the bed that was in that room and used it to cover her so she wouldn't be exposed. Layla was crying and shivering semi uncontrollably as we all looked at her in a state of shock and awe. Nana quickly came out of her room, and Big Pa rose from sitting in his chair in the living room area. They quickly came to see what happened and were in total disbelief. They both grabbed Layla and slowly walked her to the couch to wait until they got ready to drive her to the hospital that was some forty miles away. Layla would be treated for major burns across majority of her body. She had to undergo several major surgeries of skin graft. Things changed in that house after that, and another room was built to accommodate Layla's condition. When we went there to stay at Big Pa and Nana's house, we never boiled water on the stove again because a hot water heater was installed. But for no reason that I can remember, Wayne and Ross, particularly Ross, never stayed at Big Pa and Nana's again.

We eventually went home after that tragic incident involving Layla, and things just weren't the same after that. Things would also change with Mom and Dad. When we would drive to see family from that day forward, there would be a different visiting arrangement. Wayne started staying in West Daytona at Dad's sister Jordyn May's house for the summers, and I would stay at Big Pa and Nana's house a few more times. There was one time when Mom was experiencing a relapse at Big Pa and Nana's house in Dolphin, and the entire family was present. Mom would not trust anyone at all that day. Everyone was trying to give her food and water and trying to get her to take her medicine, but she refused. I thought to myself and remembered this one time when we were at home and Mom wouldn't trust any of us. For her to trust me, I ate some food and drank some water in front of her, and at that moment, I gained her trust. But by this time, we were all outside in the front yard at around 11:00 a.m., so I rushed into the house and grabbed a glass of water. I walked back outside, and without trying to look too suspicious, I walked up to Mom and began talking with her with the glass of water in my hand. While talking with her, I drank some water and then asked her if she wanted some. Mom said, "Yes." She then took the water and drank it. I was also able to get Mom to take her medication, and she eventually settled down, and she would be fine—not one hundred percent, but well enough for us to travel back home to Leesville.

Sometime after that, without notice, Dad would move out of the house, and we kids didn't know why. He would be gone for about a year and a half. We didn't know anything until Mom told us that he moved out, and later we would find out that he was now living with another woman. It appeared during this time that Mom was doing quite well. Mom was probably taking her medication regularly, and it kept her stable. Mom appeared to handle Dad's leaving and living with another woman damn well. Mom had two men coming by to check on us regularly. One man's name is Mr. Penny, and he lived in the neighborhood across the street from us and was a little bit overweight. He owned a black Lincoln car that had doors that opened toward the front of the car. He would bake Mom bread a lot and give us food. The other man, whose name I can't remember, was a very nice man. He was dark skinned, and he was the only one out of the two who I can remember coming into our house. He would play and talk with us, and he took us to our first and only live wrestling match that had famous wrestlers. That wrestling event was the most exciting thing I had ever seen live. We would travel to go see family in Dolphin, but once again, it would be different because we would travel without Dad this time. Thank god Mom was doing well, and we made it all the way on our own. Mom would first drop Ross, Farrah, and Velvet in West Daytona at the house of Dad's mom. We wouldn't call Dad's mom grandma or grandmother or granny because we were instructed to call her Cattie. We would then drive to Dolphin to Nana and Big Pa's house, and Mom would drop me and Wayne off. Mom would talk for a while and then get ready to leave, and Wayne and I would kiss and hug her and say our goodbyes.

One time, it was nighttime and pitch dark, and Mom began her travel back home to Leesville/New Contact on her own. About thirty minutes passed, and suddenly, we heard a car horn honking out front of Nana and Big Pa's house. We looked out the window, and it was Mom with the hazard lights flashing on the car. We all went outside, and Mom stepped out of the car. She was hysterical. We all asked her what was wrong, and she told us that she had just hit a cow down the street. We were stunned, and we went to look at the damage of the car. The first thing that came to my mind was that Mom was having another mental relapse, but she wasn't. During that time, we owned a yellow station wagon with brown siding called a Ford Country Squire. We looked at the driver's side of the car, and there was a major gash and dent located at the turn signal light and bumper area. There was a lot of cow manure spread all down the driver's side of the station wagon that must have sprayed out of the cow's butt when it was hit. She must have hit the cow at the head and neck area first, and then the mid and butt section of the cow swung around and hit the driver's side. It was such a mess, and it smelled so bad. Big Pa and Pete got into Big Pa's truck and drove to see the accident's site. They came back and said the cow was dead. I am not sure if the police were called or not, but Big Pa did know who owned the cow and informed them of what happened. The owner was not surprised that one of his cows had gotten outside of the fenced area. The station wagon was still drivable, and the next morning, Big Pa took it to the car wash to clean it. Mom would drive back home by herself later that day and contact Dad and to tell him of the accident so he could report it to the insurance company. I am not sure how he took the news of the accident, but I am sure he was not happy and not surprised that something would happen with her. For all we know, he may have thought she caused the accident on purpose to somehow keep communications open with him.

During that summer visit, I would become the proud owner of a crow. Yes, I said a crow. One day, just like any other day, around 10:00

a.m., I went to walk about fifty yards to the main street and check the mail for Nana. It was a beautiful, sunny morning, and that day, right when I took the mail out of the mailbox, this black crow landed on the mailbox. It scared me so badly that I tossed the mail up in the air, and I took off running back to the house. As I ran, the crow flew right alongside me, and I thought it was going to attack me. I ran into the house, shut the screen door, and looked out. The crow landed on a swing set that was in the front yard. The crow just stayed there, and I decided to go outside and try something. Once I walked off the porch, I called for the crow to come to me. I said, "Come here, crow," and suddenly the crow flew over to me and landed on my shoulder. It scared the living daylights out of me, yet I was amazed it worked. The crow and I became friends, and we were inseparable. That crow and I did everything together. The crow would clean its beak against my shoulder, swiping left and then right. It would fly to the trees and come back to me when I called it. It would eat right out of my hand, and I would feed it corn, peas, and watermelon. It really liked watermelon. And the surprising, special thing about the crow was that the crow could talk. It would say, "Hello, goodbye and how are you" and its speech was very clear. At nighttime, when I went to bed, the crow would stay outside the house in the trees and wait for me the next morning. It was the best experience for a young boy like me. That crow was the best thing that could have happened to me. When it came time for us to drive to Bible study in town, surprisingly, the crow flew along with the car and went to church with me. The crow was outside waiting obviously, but I couldn't wait for Bible study to end. When I went outside, the crow was right there waiting for me. We went back home, and the crow flew back right along the car with us. One morning, the entire family was amazed by this relationship I had with this crow that they came outside to see, but it didn't go too well because when my cousin Layla came outside to see the crow, it attacked her. It went right to her feet and pecked her feet, and Nana did not like that at all. Layla's left foot was bleeding a little bit. I yelled at the crow, and it came back to me. Well the next day, when it was time to go to Bible study again, Nana asked me to call the crow to come to me, and I did. Right at that time, Nana grabbed the crow. The crow was flapping its wings hard, trying to get away. It was trying to peck at Nana's hand and arm, but Nana held on tight, and she quickly walked over to the chicken coop that was on the left side of the house. She put my crow in it. The crow would caw and caw and jump up and down until we drove out of sight to attend Bible study. We went home later than usual, and by the time we got home, it was pitch dark. I jumped out of the car and ran to the chicken coop, calling the crow, but it was not there, it was gone. The first thing that came to my mind was that maybe a snake climbed into the coop and ate it, but there was no sign of the crow. I called for the crow a few more times, and after no response, I went into the house. I was heartbroken. I got up early the next morning and went back to the chicken coop, and I saw no sign of struggle. I concluded that the crow eventually got out somehow and flew away looking for me, and when it didn't find me, it probably flew back to where it came from. I would never see that crow again. I would look up into the sky and see lots of crows flying by, and I would call, but none of them would respond. I would continue that routine every day until it was time to go back home to New Contact. I had already thought about what kind of cage I was going to get to bring it back home with me. I was sad for a few days. I didn't even want to go to Bible study anymore. By now it was so boring, and there was nothing there to do except walk around and play in the ditches, and, on occasion, I would find different types of turtles. One day, everybody left the house, and I was there all by myself because for some reason, Wayne had stopped staying there with me. One boring day, I did something really stupid—I decided to go streaking. I took off all my clothes and ran out the front door butt-ass naked. I ran to the right side of the house all the way to the back and successfully made it to the back door. I felt so victorious, like I had accomplished something weirdly incredible—at least I thought I was successful, until I reached up to grab the metal handle to open the rear screen door, and to my surprise, it was locked. My jaw dropped to the ground, and my eyes popped out of my head. I know at that moment that I did not think to unlock the rear screen door before because I simply thought it was already unlocked in the first place. Immediately I said to myself, "What if they are back and out front?" I slowly looked around the corner of the house from where I came and saw no one. I took off sprinting like I was Jesse Owens and made it back to the front door relieved. I never did something stupid like that again, and that would be the last time I would stay at Nana and Big Pa's house.

Now, at the time of writing this book, I am thinking that after forty years, it never occurred to me why Nana didn't like my crow. Nana probably thought the crow was a bad omen, especially since it attacked Layla. There were three other females that came outside to see my crow when Layla got pecked. Why would it only attack Layla? Mom would eventually come back and get all of us from our various locations, and we would go back home. After Mom had the cow accident with the car, Wayne and I would never stay at Big Pa and Nana's house again. Wayne and I started staying with my dad's sister, Jordyn May Rock. Jordyn May's house was about ten feet away from our grandma Cattie's house, which was located on Jackman Street in West Daytona, Texas. I was either sixteen or seventeen years old when Wayne and I started staying with our aunt Jordyn May for the summer. One summer, I got a job as a roofer. I would lay tar paper, set shingles, and hammer them to the roof with nails. It was a great summer job, and I loved it because I made good amount of money, and I had a lot of fun staying with my cousins. One day, like routine, I heated up pots of water to take a bath—yes, even at my aunt's house. I filled the pot to the very top and brought it to a boil. And wouldn't you know it, our family history of burning ourselves with hot boiling water would not bypass me. I went to pick up the pot of water so I could walk and empty it into the tub, but I made a mistake. I was holding the pot way too high up past my waist, and before I could take more than about three steps, I rocked the pot of hot boiling water and spilled it on myself. I stopped moving immediately because I was in shock and a lot of pain. I quickly walked to the bathroom and emptied the pot of boiling water into the tub, and I sat the pot on the ground and went and closed the door. The pain was excruciating, and I unzipped and pulled my pants down to look at the burned area. I saw steam coming off my pants and legs. One of my cousins knew what had happened to me, and I asked him to go get me a stick of cool butter, and then I sat down on the toilet so I could see exactly where I had been burned. I was burned primarily on the front of my right thigh. I also had burned a small area on the front of my left thigh, and I also burned my penis. Of all the damn places to get burned, I burned my damn penis. Next, I took that whole bar of butter, tore part of the wrapper off, and started rubbing the butter on my legs and penis. The butter felt so cool, and it was soothing. After rubbing butter on those three areas, I began to laugh at myself. I was thinking to myself that if my friends and family could see me rubbing butter on my damn penis, they would laugh their asses off, but my laughter did not last long because the pain was so excruciating that I almost couldn't stand it. And wouldn't you know it, I looked up, and one of my cousins was in between the two houses looking through a crack in the wall, laughing at me spreading butter on my penis and legs. The burned areas blistered up over the next couple of days, and I rubbed a lot of burn ointment on them, but none seemed to work until I tried an ointment called Campho-Phenique. That ointment worked like a champ and seemed like it healed my burns within a week's time. Before the Campho-Phenique ointment, I had been bedridden for a few days because I couldn't put pants or shorts on. Back in that day, shorts weren't baggy like they are now. If I had put on shorts of that time, it would have looked like I was wearing booty shorts, and that was not going to happen. To this day I still use Campho-Phenique. The summer would eventually end, and we would go back home to Leesville.

Wayne and I would get into some legal trouble once we settled back at home in Leesville. We were involved in a large theft ring of stealing bicycles in our neighborhood. We were with five other kids—Randall and Wilbur Watson, Kevin Partner, David, and one other kid. Wayne stole one bike one night. I never stole one bike, but I was with them on two occasions. Between the seven of us, about fifty bikes were stolen over a month. We didn't get caught by the police because of the bikes, but got caught because of breaking and entering. The ringleader was a kid named Kevin Partner. Kevin had broken into this house that he said was abandoned. He said the military man had taken his wife to California for mental treatment and that the military man wouldn't be back for months. I was told of the house after some of the guys had already been in the house for a few days. One day, only five of us went into the house and took some items. I took a nice pair of boots and a nice coin. The house was located right on the edge of the woods, so we went out the back door and walked to the woods to store the items by some trees. Shockingly, on our way out of the woods, I looked at the man's house and noticed a car in the driveway. We were all scared and immediately went home. A few days later, the police came to our houses and took us to the city hall in handcuffs. Later, we had to appear in court, and my brother and I were placed on probation. After only two months, we were released off probation, and we credit the move to another state and the fact that Wayne wrote and pleaded with the probation officer to release us because it was our first offense and we were good kids.

Meanwhile, Mom was fighting her battle with Dad. Somehow, Mom received more information about the woman he was seeing and found out the lady's name and where she lived. Dad was now living with this lady full time, and her name was Margaret Stevens. Mom would drive us past her house on occasion to see if Dad's car was parked at her place. Knowing Dad, he probably parked his car behind her house. Mom used to tell us that Margaret Stevens put voodoo on Dad, and she was convinced of that. Mom would say that Margaret Stevens pissed in a glass jar and buried it in her yard, and that kept Dad there and was the reason why he would not leave her and come back home to live with us. Mom would make attempts to call him, but he would not answer her calls. Since she was not getting anywhere with just calling him, she decided to pack us all in the car and drive to the Fort Conquest Army Post, where Dad was staying in some living quarters. We walked into some recreational area with a pool table, and Mom and Dad talked. Mom was pleading with him to come back home, and he was not hearing it. The whole time we were there, Dad did not hug us, kiss us, or ask us how we were doing. We left with no resolution.

Because Wayne and I were getting older and starting to get too big for our own britches and needed to stay positively occupied, Mom put us into a recreational center for kids on post. A military bus would even pick us up every weekend and bring us home after a few hours. The place was called the YAC, which stands for Youth Activity Center, and it was great because it kept our minds off what was happening with Mom and Dad, and we could play with our friends. Mom would remain stable in her mental state, and things would go well until one day, we heard the "D" word for the first time. Mom and Dad told us that they were getting a divorce. It was real and devastating for us, and unfortunately, Dad had started divorce proceedings sometime in early 1976, after sixteen years of marriage. In May, Dad received papers to go to his next duty station of Rushmore/Fort Gold, Texas. We kids were overly sad about the divorce, and on top of that, we were moving away from our friends of six years. Even though a divorce was filed, Dad still had to move his family with him because he was still legally married to Mom. He probably didn't like that too much since he had a girlfriend and probably didn't want to leave her. Eventually we would pack up the house, load up the 1975 Ford Country Squire, and head for Rushmore/Fort Gold, Texas. And by the way, Dad got the station wagon repaired from the accident with the cow.

CHAPTER SIX

Dad gets stationed at Fort Gold, Texas; we live in Rushmore; Mom's behavior is seriously unstable; I get sprayed with Mace

We moved to Rushmore/Fort Gold, Texas, and almost immediately, Dad received orders to go to Korea. We weren't sure when he would leave, but it would be soon, within the next few weeks. We found our new house located at 806 Noah Street. The city of Rushmore was connected to Fort Gold. The house we moved into was a brown three-bedroom duplex. Wayne, Ross, and I shared a room, and Farrah and Velvet shared a room. Ross and I had a bunk bed in which I slept on top, and Wayne had a bed all to himself. Soon, Wayne and I would continue our feud just like we had in New Contact and have our first major disagreement, which resulted in a whipping for both of us delivered by Dad. I really did not like Dad after that whipping and had thoughts just like all kids have after they get in trouble with a parent—thoughts like him getting hit by a car, or that something would happen to him. Really, it was my fault. The next day came, and Wayne and I put aside our differences. We wanted to see the neighborhood, so we took off walking around just to check it out, and after only walking for about ten minutes, we looked across the street and saw some friends, Leroy and Daniel Roberts from Fort Conquest, Louisiana. They were walking and looking around like we were. We went over, greeted, and hugged them, and we were so excited to have some friends we knew. They lived just about two blocks away at 608 Harbor Street. For now, things seemed to go well at home, except Wayne and Mom continued their confrontations, and it put a strain on the rest of us. It appeared to me that the reason that Wayne and Mom were not getting along was me. Wayne was getting in trouble—in Mom's eyes—quite often. I can't remember why Wayne and I didn't get along, but maybe it had something to do with Mom's mental condition because Mom and I had a great relationship, and Wayne was jealous of it. In any case, Mom's condition would get worse.

One day, Mom got on Wayne quite sternly and told him to leave me alone and stop messing with me. Even when we lived in Louisiana, Wayne got reprimanded by Mom about me, so that night, I really felt bad. Late that night, I went into the kitchen, grabbed a butcher knife, and took it to bed with me. I went up on my top bunk and put the knife to my wrist but couldn't cut myself because Mom's reminder rang out in my mind about not committing suicide. I never attempted or thought of doing that again. Now the time had come for Dad to leave for Korea, but as I am writing this book, I just find out from my dad that he went to Korea in September 1976. We arrived in Rushmore in June 1976, so where was Dad between June and September? Since our parents were getting a divorce, Dad had no reason to stick around, not even for us kids. Dad probably felt bad and embarrassed about being with another woman and divorcing Mom, so most likely he went back to Louisiana to spend time with his girlfriend Margaret Stevens before he left for Korea. Now that Dad was gone, Wayne was in a leadership role that carried a lot of responsibility since he was the oldest. But Wayne was taking on a serious problem with Mom's mental condition, in which he had no training or any experience whatsoever. If Dad walked out on Mom and he was an adult, there was no way Wayne could handle that enormous task of handling Mom as a teenager. Wayne was irritated and impatient, and I could see that he was at a loss for words on what to do about Mom's behavior. Wayne would yell and demand that Mom do what he said, and Mom would not have it because he was the child and she was the adult. Wayne did the best he could, but the tension between him and Mom just got worse.

Several months passed, and Mom's behavior was rapidly declining. We must get help for us and Mom. I am not sure how the word got out to Dad's superiors in the army, but it did, and his service in Korea was cut short. He was forced to come back home to take care of Mom and us because a divorce decree had not been issued. In the days before Dad came back home, Mom's behavior grew more bizarre and scary. The only comfort we had was an album that Mom would play over and over, as it soothed her. We thought it was strange hearing this album play over and over until we listened to the words. The words were uplifting and inspiring. I was not sure where and what store she got the album from, or even if she went to the record store and purchased it herself, or if someone gave it to her, but as far as Farrah and I were concerned, the record was given to our mother from Almighty God. The album was a recording by the artist and songstress named Ms. Candi Staton, and the name of the album was *Young Hearts Run Free*. That album was the grace that God sent us, soothing Mom and giving Farrah and me complete comfort after we understood the words. That record played day and night, and it helped us. It was like God was speaking to us all through that album. Within a few days, we got word from some army personnel that Dad was on his way back from Korea and that it would take him about a day or two to return. Meanwhile, we would maintain the day-to-day routine, trying to console and comfort Mom. She would sleep an hour here and an hour there. All of us kids appeared to take Mom's condition in stride because we had seen it before. A few days later, Dad arrived, and when I heard of his return, it was late in the evening, around eight o'clock. I was not home when he arrived because I was out with my friends. Dad drove around town looking for me, and he found me walking down Wiley Street with my friends Gavin Metals and George Treat. Dad told me to get in the car with him so we could go home and figure out what we were going to do with Mom. It was a silent ride home. Dad tried to talk to me, but I didn't have much to say, for I was trying to get used to him being around again. Dad appeared glad to be back and glad that he found me by the look on his face. I remember that first night he was back. It was very awkward, but the awkwardness would soon be overshadowed by Mom's behavior. One of the first things Dad did when he got home was call for help from Nana and Big Pa, who raised Mom. Big Pa told Dad that they would be on their way.

Things appeared to go well because we were a family again, and that was what Mom wanted, so she was trying to behave and get sleep. That worked for about a day because her behavior would not get better. It really started spiraling out of control. The next morning started off calm and positive because Dad had cooked a big breakfast of grits, bacon, toast, pancakes, and orange juice. It was really nice, but Mom was not buying it, and she would not eat or drink anything. Once again, I remembered the technique I used when Mom was sick at Nana and Big Pa's house, when I got Mom to trust me with my glass of water. I went into the kitchen and got a glass of water, and I went to her sitting in the living room. I stood in front of her and asked her if she wanted some water. I took a big gulp of the water, and she saw me drinking it. She took the glass of water out of my hand and drank all of it herself. She gave me back the glass and said, "Thank you, dear." I then made her a plate of food, ate some of it in front of her, and asked her if she wanted some, and she said yes. I then went on to feed her, and she ate all the food and said to me, "You are a kind son, thank you." At that moment, I felt like a million bucks.

Well, the night came, and it brought some of the most bizarre behavior and phenomena I had ever witnessed. First in a chain of events was when Wayne and Mom were at odds and arguing, and this time Wayne flexed his own muscles. Wayne was tired of Mom's behavior and just wanted her to act right, so he went into our bedroom, grabbed a baseball bat, and came back and got in Mom's face. They stood face to face, and he raised the baseball bat with one hand and threatened to hit her with it. Wayne told Mom that if she did not go sit down, he was going to hit her upside the head with the bat. Dad quickly intervened, stayed calm, took the bat from Wayne, and told him to go sit down. Mom said things to Dad, telling him that Jesus was there and she would raise one hand high in the air and yell, "Prince of Peace, help me!" And she told Dad that he should not be with Margaret Stevens. Mom said more bizarre things, and Dad did not get upset—he remained calm, laughed, and made light of the things she was saying.

The next thing in the chain of events was when Dad finally got Mom to sit down on the couch, and while we were all looking at her, she said that the Prince of Peace was there. She told the Prince of Peace to sit down next to her. As I was looking at Mom sitting on the couch, I saw the spot next to her scrunch down, as if someone had just sat down next to her. I am not sure if anyone else saw what I saw, but I knew that it was real and that something spiritual was happening that night. I felt comforted by what appeared to me to be the presence of the Prince of Peace, and during that time, I had no idea what or who the Prince of Peace was. Some ten years later, I found out that it was another name for our Lord and Savior Jesus Christ.

Just like the Bible says, whenever you do good, evil is always present, and this next thing in the chain of events will prove that. A little time passed by, and Mom was constantly going at it with Dad. At that time, Mom was wearing a pink nightgown, and suddenly she stood up, pulled down her panties to her knees, placed the Bible on the ground between her legs, and urinated on it. We were all in shock and disbelief as we witnessed this bizarre behavior right before our eyes. Dad went and got a towel and placed it on the Bible to sop up the urine. Suddenly, we heard a knock at the door, and it was Big Pa and cousin Thomas James. Mom was so happy to see them. Mom really loved them both because they had always treated her good, plus they were her own real family. Big Pa and Thomas James dealt with Mom's behavior with such patience, care, and love, and they had mastered how to deal with her. Mom always calmed down whenever she saw Big Pa and Thomas James, and they could talk to her in ways no one else could. Big Pa also had another nickname, and it was Sugar Bear. Mom adored him. They sat down, had a few beers, and talked for about an hour; Mom was extremely calm and relaxed. I never saw moments of distress during their visits. Right at the end of that hour, an ambulance showed up in the driveway. Big Pa and Thomas James convinced Mom to get into the ambulance, and they took her to the hospital to be assessed. Mom would eventually be transported to the state hospital located in Austin, Texas. Nana didn't come because she couldn't make long trips and sit in one spot for long periods at a time anymore, as she had been in two or three head-on car collisions over the years. Big Pa and cousin Thomas James went to a hotel for the night and said they would come back tomorrow morning. The morning came, and Big Pa and Thomas James came back. Dad told them that he would be moving us on to post housing, and they took most of Mom's items with them because Dad had no more use for them. They said their goodbyes and drove back home to Dolphin.

About two weeks passed by, and Dad had already planned a trip to go see Mom at the state hospital in Austin, Texas. We all loaded up into the car and drove to Austin. We arrived at the state hospital, and once again we drove into a gated and guarded community. The landscape had beautiful trees and flowers, and there were lots of squirrels everywhere. Dad went into the front office, and the attendant summoned Mom and told her that she had visitors. Mom came out and looked sedated. She looked rested and tired at the same time. I really thought she would never leave that place this time because her behavior was so bizarre. After about an hour, we ended our visit and drove back home to Rushmore. By now, Dad was in full parent mode and had to provide and do all things for us as parents had to do. Dad decided that Wayne had to move from the house after that bat-threatening incident with Mom, and he would live with Dad's sister Jordyn May and attend school in West Daytona, Texas, at Daytona High School—the same high school that Mom and Dad attended. I would enroll at Wiley Junior High, which had grades seven, eight, and nine. My other siblings would be enrolled in elementary school.

Our parents' divorce became final, and Dad was granted full custody of us. Before long, Farrah did something which Dad didn't like, and it made him really mad. It made him mad enough that he whipped her. Keep in mind that Farrah was now about fifteen years old and had a lot of attitude. It had been such a long time since Dad had whipped any of us, and that whipping really scared me because Dad had big muscles and was very strong. Anyhow, he whipped the hell out of her. I took off running out of the house and down the street. I wasn't looking for help, I just needed to get out of there. After running about a block or two,

I stopped, turned around, and slowly walked back home. I don't even think Dad knew I left the house. Things eventually settled down, and we began getting reacquainted with our father. I got my very first job working at a hamburger place across the street from Wiley Junior High's football field. About a month later, Farrah and I found out that Mom had been discharged from the state hospital and was back in Rushmore living in an apartment across the street from Rushmore High School.

By now, school had ended for the summer, and we were to take a trip to visit family in West Daytona, but Dad had other plans, and we ended up staying there for most of the summer. It was a lot of fun hanging with my brother and cousins. I would date a beautiful, petite girl with beautiful straight black hair who lived in a trailer about a block from my aunt's house. Her name was Ashley May Crown. She was the first girl I had sex with. Good thing she had a condom, because I didn't have one, as I wasn't the type of boy to have random sex, much less have sex, period. I wanted to wait until I got married to have sex, but she gave me the condom. I tried to put it on instead of roll it on, and I messed it up, so we didn't use it. Meanwhile, Dad was moving our family on to the army post to live in military housing. Summer ended, and then it came time to go back home. We went directly to our new house in Fort Gold. In the fall of 1978, I registered at Rushmore High School for tenth grade, and I also registered to play football for the Rushmore Kangaroos as the starting JV running back. By now, Mom had relocated and moved to the city of Dallas to a very nice upstairs apartment. We missed her a lot, and Farrah and I wanted to visit her, so we got in contact with my favorite cousins, David Lee and Fiona Branch. Fiona and her husband met us, and they took us to where Mom was living. We had a great visit. Mom was a little standoffish but welcomed us into her beautifully decorated apartment. The visit was short, and we went back home. It seemed scary that Mom would live in Dallas all by herself, but she said she was not afraid and that she loved the big city. Sometime later, Mom told us that she was moving to Alaska to live with her aunt Scarlet Dodge, who sent for her. Aunt Scarlet also told Mom that if she moved to Alaska, she wouldn't get sick anymore because God told her that. Mom flew to Alaska, and for twenty straight years, she didn't have any major mental lapses, but I will talk about that part of the story later.

It was now 1978, and Dad moved the family on the post of Fort Gold, specifically in the Comanche 3 housing area. We moved into a large two-story duplex that seemed like a house. I had my own room, Ross had his own room, and Farrah and Velvet shared a room. It was like living in paradise, and this was the first time we had ever lived on an army post. Our house was connected to another house, and the family there would become our friends. The family had two daughters that we grew to like a whole lot, and their names were Faith and Hope. What a coincidence that their names would be Faith and Hope. God and his angels were with us most of the places we went. Several unusual things happened in that house on post, and Mom wasn't even with us. Dad got involved with a lady who caught him with another woman, and she devised a plan to get back at him. One night, Dad and one of his lady friends named Lauren were sitting in lawn chairs in the front yard, drinking, talking, and just enjoying each other's company. Farrah and I were in the house talking about how awkward the relationship was because that lady Dad was with was the mother of some good friend of ours from when we lived in Louisiana. While we were sitting in the living room watching television, the telephone rang, and it was Cheryl, one of Dad's other girlfriends who he had been dating for a while. Yeah, Dad was a player and was seeing two women at the same time. Cheryl asked me and Farrah to come up the road from the house to talk to her, so we turned the TV off and walked up the street about five houses away from ours and spoke with her. She wanted to know if Dad was at the house with another woman. Farrah and I looked at each other and were hesitant to answer because we felt a little uncomfortable, but innocently we said that he was. Cheryl asked us what her name was, and we said, "Lauren, she's a friend of the family." Dad and Lauren became friends after Dad had returned from Korea. Dad was friends with Lauren's husband T. J. Roberts when they were in Korea together. Dad told us that T. J. told him to look up his wife Lauren when he got back to the States, and he sure did. Wayne and I knew T. J. and Lauren's sons Leroy and Daniel from when we lived in Leesville, and we considered one another as family. Well, Cheryl was mad as hell, but we didn't know it at the time. She asked us to walk her down to the house because she wanted to talk to Dad and Lauren. Cheryl left her car unlocked, and we proceeded to walk down the hill to the house. We got to the front yard, and Cheryl walked and stood directly in front of Dad and Lauren. They remained in their seats while Cheryl addressed her concerns. Cheryl said, "Hello, Bruce," and without warning, Cheryl pulled this small can of spray from behind her and immediately started spraying it on Dad and Lauren. This spray was Mace. The wind was blowing strong that evening, and the Mace blew right back into Farrah and my direction, getting into our eyes and throat. I am not sure how much Cheryl sprayed, but it seemed like a lot. I know I was temporarily blind and couldn't breathe well. Farrah and I took off running in the opposite direction of the spray. I could barely see but saw Cheryl running and chasing after Dad and Lauren all over the yard with the Mace. It was terrible. My eyes and throat were burning, tears were running from my eyes, and my nose was beginning to clog with snot. I called out to Farrah, and we got together and ran up the street to my friend Wayne Atom's house. We used his front yard water hose to wash out our eyes. After about thirty or forty minutes, we went back home and saw that Lauren's car was still in our driveway. Farrah and I walked around to the back of the house because we were afraid to go into the house. When we got to the back of the house, we heard some people talking from inside, in the living room area. We listened from outside the window and heard Lauren questioning and hitting Dad at the same time. We could tell Dad was getting punched by Lauren. Dad never raised his voice or manhandled her. He just took his punishment like a man. The humility Dad showed from Lauren hitting him also showed me that Dad was not being fake about being patient when he dealt with my mother as well. Sometime later that night, Cheryl called Farrah and me to apologize to us for what happened, and we never saw Cheryl again.

It was late 1979, and I was hired to work at Western Sizzlin' Steakhouse. This was my second real job, and I loved it. My first real job I worked at Bonanza Restaurant, and the manager there was C. L. Scott. He was offered the position as store manager at Western Sizzlin', and when he left Bonanza, he asked me to go with him to Western Sizzlin', so I followed him there. He was so fair, nice, and kind, and he treated me with a lot of respect and dignity. He was a great man, and he allowed me to live with him for a short time. He even gave me permission to drive the company car leased by Western Sizzlin'. What was even more surprising was that he said it was okay to drive his very own Datsun 280ZX sports car. C. L. Scott was one of the greatest men I had ever known, and I did not mind working my ass off for him. I would eventually buy my own car because I did not want him to think I was taking advantage of him. Shortly after the completion of another high school in Rushmore called C. E. Guthridge High School, I was forced to attend Guthridge High School in 1979 because of zone boundaries. I eventually graduated early from that high school in February 1980, and after that, I ventured off on a pilgrimage across Texas with my sister Farrah, my girlfriend Tiffany Dane, and a large stuffed teddy bear in my 1976 Ford Elite. We traveled from Rushmore/Fort Gold to Port Arthur, and then to Dallas, and then to West Daytona, and then back to Dallas in a week's time. My sister eventually flew to be with our mother in the latter part of 1980, and me and my girlfriend found an apartment in Dallas and lived across the street from the famous Stratus dome. My girlfriend and I had our first child out of wedlock in June 1981, but having a kid did not fill the strong desire to be close to my mother so I could help her. That desire was overwhelming, so I decided that my family would move to Alaska. I packed up my little family, purchased three tickets to ride the Greyhound bus, and we traveled for two days from Dallas to Seattle, Washington, and then we took a flight on Western Airlines and arrived in Anchorage, Alaska, on October 17, 1981.

CHAPTER SEVEN

I make a pilgrimage to join my mother in Anchorage,
Alaska in October of 1981; Farrah stabs her boyfriend

My girlfriend, my daughter, and I arrived in Anchorage,
Alaska, on October 17, 1981, and I loved it from the
moment I stepped off the plane. We were greeted in the
airport by my sister, her all thumbs boyfriend Roger Stone, and of course,
my loving mother. I can't explain the excitement and heart-filling joy
in seeing my mother. She never looked so beautiful, and Alaska agreed
with her. She simply loved Alaska, as she said with her own words. Now
Mom was reunited with two of her children, and three more needed
to be reunited. Right away, we got reacquainted with each other, but
Mom really took a fondness for my daughter, her first grandchild, as
she always said. Mom had her own place, and we lived with her in that
one-bedroom apartment. Farrah and her live-in boyfriend had their
own apartment, and they lived in the same apartment complex but one
section over and downstairs from us. I needed to find a job right away
to care for my new family, and I was more than confident and assured
I would find a job. But my assurance faded slowly but surely because
six months passed by, and I was not able to land a job of any sort. I was
encouraged to go to the welfare office downtown to get some form of
help. I got up first thing the following Monday and caught the city bus
to the downtown welfare office. I arrived around 9:00 a.m., and the

line was out the door and twenty people long, all waiting to get help. I immediately said "Forget it," turned around, and went back home, but I told myself that I would go back the next day earlier. The next day, Tuesday, I did the same routine, and when I arrived at the welfare office, it was 8:00 a.m. This time, the line was out the door thirty people long, but I stayed, got in the line, and waited it out. I made it to speak to a social worker six hours later, and I handed the social worker my paperwork. She stamped it, filed it, and told me my appointment to see if I qualify would be forty-five days from then. I said, "You have got to be kidding me. I have to come back in forty-five days just to see if I qualify?"

She then said, "Yes, and that is all I can do for you now, but if you want to come back much earlier tomorrow morning and be one of the first fourteen people in line, then you would be assessed if you qualify for assistance and would receive benefits that same day."

After she told me that, I was elated, and then I asked, "How early should I get here?"

"Very early, like 5:00 or 6:00 a.m."

"Really?"

"If you don't, I guess you don't need help that badly."

I looked at her with a determined look on my face, left the Welfare office, went home, and had some dinner while coming up with my plan to leave at 4:00 am. I would have to walk because the city bus transit system didn't run at that time, and the welfare office was about ten miles away. I went to bed early and set my alarm. The alarm went off at 4:00 a.m., and I got dressed, prayed, and started walking in twenty-five-degree temperature. The roads and sidewalks were icy and snowy, and after only about thirty minutes, I started to get cold. The roads were quiet with no moving vehicles in sight, so I decided to pray to God to send me a ride, and after ten minutes, an orange checker cab approached me, and I decided to stick out my thumb to see if I could hitch a ride. I then said to myself, "If this cab driver is white, I can forget it because he will not pick up my black ass in the middle of the night. Who would have the nerve to pick up a twenty-year-old black man at four in the morning? Not me." But I stuck my thumb out anyway and said another prayer. The checker cab started to slow down, and to my surprise, the driver stopped the cab in front of me. The driver was a white male in his late fifties. He rolled down the passenger-side window and asked me if I needed a ride, and I said, "Yes, but I don't have any money, and I am on my way to the welfare office." He said, "This early in the morning?" I further explained that I needed help for me and my family, and he said, "Get in." I was so elated. I got into the cab and said thank you. On the way to the office, I explained that I moved to Alaska from Dallas, Texas, six months ago, and I had a girlfriend and a baby girl. I had not been able to find a job to provide food for us. I told him that the reason I was up so early on my way to the welfare office was so that I could be one of the first fourteen people in line. He said that was awesome of me and asked me a few more questions about myself, and fifteen to twenty minutes later, we arrived at the welfare office. I overly expressed my gratitude for the ride and wished that one day I could pay him back. I got out of the cab and walked toward the front door of the welfare office when suddenly, I heard the cab's horn blow. I looked back at the cab, and the cab driver waved for me to come back. I then went back, and when I got there, he reached out to hand me a big wad of money and said, "Take it, and I will not take no for an answer. Take care of your girlfriend and that new baby girl of yours." And then he quickly drove away. I was not able to get his name or cab number, and I never saw him again.

I walked over to the front door of the welfare office and was the second person in line. I counted the money, and it totaled almost two hundred dollars. I instantly started crying. I cried for three reasons: the first one was that I was going to get some help that day, the second was that I had no money at all and that cab driver fixed that, and third, I didn't know how to pay him back because I didn't know who he was. I was so grateful for his gesture. I decided to exalt the Lord in thanks and praise. I left the welfare office with the help I needed and took the city bus back home. I shared my abundance of great news with my family.

My miracles, as I call them now, would be overshadowed by one of our family's first incidents. One late night, at about 1:00 a.m., I was lying in my bed, which was a three-blanket pallet on the floor. I was listening to the radio program KCKA Flight Heart for Heart FM 91.1 with DJ Mattson Jewels and Hardy James aka Mitchell Cantone. I saw red light flashing and reflecting off the wall. I got up to look outside, and I saw police cars and an ambulance. I said to Mom, "Mom there are police and an ambulance out front. I sure hope they are not here for Farrah and Roger." Well I put some clothes on, and I walked downstairs to the adjacent door to where Farrah and Roger lived. I saw the police at the front door, which was open. I walk through the front door, and there was Roger strapped to a gurney. I saw a whole bunch of blood on the living room floor. I asked what happened, and Farrah came from the bedroom and said, "I stabbed Roger a little bit in his arm." The paramedics said that Roger would be fine and that they were transporting him to the hospital. I asked Farrah what happened and why she stabbed him. She said, "Roger and I were arguing, and then Roger pushed me, and my night gown flew up and his uncle Stan saw me naked." Stan was Roger's uncle who was staying with them. Roger received several stitches for his stab wound, but he was going to be fine. The police asked Roger if he wanted to press charges against Farrah, and he said no. Roger came home that same night and was all right. Mom acted as if she was not surprised by Farrah's and Roger's behavior, and she said that they fought quite often.

A few months later, Farrah and I got into a fight because I told her she should treat Roger better, and she didn't like that. She came up to our apartment and got in my face like she wanted to fight me, and she told me I could not tell her what to do and to stay out of her business. She came close to assaulting me, and I pushed her down the stairs about eight steps to the ground floor. She got extremely furious with me, and she ran out of the building, went to her apartment, and ran back carrying a large butcher knife. I immediately closed the door. She stood outside the door cursing and threatening me. She eventually went home, and I didn't see or speak to her for a long time. Mom's apartment was too small for the four of us, so we moved about a mile away to another one-bedroom but larger living space. Soon, Farrah and Roger moved to a duplex almost across the street from where they were at.

It was around September 1982, and Farrah and I had not spoken to each other for months, but another incident would be in the horizon and would change that. Farrah and I were forced to talk to each other because Mom was showing signs of having a nervous breakdown again. Now that we were living in Alaska, the name of Mom's condition changed to bipolar disorder with schizophrenia and paranoia. One day, Mom was attending church at Ezekiel Missionary Baptist Church with some of her church friends. Her friends caught my attention because they had noticed that Mom was acting quite differently. I was forced to end my silence with Farrah and tell her what was going on because I needed her help. We agreed to meet at the church. We confronted Mom, and she had a look in her eyes that we had grown accustomed to and could never forget because we had grown up with that look. Mom's pupils always looked large and hazed over brown and dilated. To me and Farrah, it was a very recognizable sign that told us she was just after the middle stages of a nervous breakdown. As I have now learned, it was not a nervous breakdown but something much more. But because of our inexperience, we felt like we could still try to get Mom to listen to us, and she would take her medication, get some rest, and be fine, but that was not the case. We did drive Mom home and tried our best to get her to go to sleep and get some rest, but our efforts were futile, and for the next two to three hours, Mom acted suspicious, agitated, and restless, and she refused to go to sleep. She threatened us and accused us of things we weren't doing. She looked at us strangely, but most of her attacks were directed at Farrah. Mom did not bother me that much and would be somewhat loving to me because I showed genuine care and patience for her. The incident was a lot harder than we had imagined, and we were forced to called Dad for help. Dad said Mom was off her medication, and his advice was that we needed to get her to the hospital any way we can. Dad further said that the doctors at Fort Conquest and at Pineville said that Mom would be fine as long as she took her medicine, but from what we could tell, she had stopped taking it. We needed to get her to the hospital as soon as possible. All the times before, when we were kids, Dad would use his expertise to get Mom to the hospital, but now the students had graduated and were now leading the charge to help our mother. Mom's condition would get worse and worse. Dad had asked us if there was a state mental hospital in Anchorage, and we said we weren't sure, but we would look for one in the yellow pages. We found one right in Anchorage, and it was not far from the house. The state hospital was named the Alaska Psychiatric Institute, also known as the API. We thanked Dad for his help and said goodbye. The next thing Farrah and I knew, all we had to do was to pray together. Farrah, Roger, and I prayed for assistance from the Lord. After we finished praying, we went to Mom and asked her to get in the car with us. Several times Mom said no, but after about an hour, miraculously, she did. She walked on her own with some reserve and hesitation, but eventually she would get into the car. Now, there had been many times before when we had seen Mom driven away in an ambulance to the state hospital, but this time was different. The baton had now been passed to Farrah and me, and for the first time, we were without Dad. We were on our own and taking our mother to the state hospital so she can get some help. We make it to the API without a hitch, but the intake process to get Mom admitted was a little difficult because she was not willing to go. During that whole process, Mom was attacking Farrah. No matter what Farrah did to help Mom, she attacked her in any way she could, calling Farrah names and saying that she was fat, that she wasn't treating her husband well, and that she was a bad wife. But Farrah took the insults like a champion. She did very well in ignoring Mom's attacks. We made it into the lobby, and Mom walked right back out the front doors. We persuaded her to come back in, and then she walked back out again. And that process took about thirty minutes before API workers entered the lobby with the lead nurse, and once she arrived, she showed great patience and understanding and was extremely nice. She made Mom feel so comfortable and secure that Mom just walked right in with her. Mom didn't even turn around to say goodbye to me, Farrah, or Roger, but we were oh so relieved, happy, and exhausted all at the same time because we had been trying to get Mom into the API for half a day.

I went to the apartment that I shared with Mom and greeted my girlfriend and daughter who were waiting for me. Roger and Farrah went to their apartment. I was so tired that I laid down immediately, and as soon as my head hit the pillow, I fell asleep. A couple of hours passed, and when the telephone rang, I was reluctant to answer because I was so tired, but I did anyway, and I was glad I did. It was the head nurse of the mental ward from the API. The head nurse said that they tried everything to get Mom to settle down and to take some medication, but their efforts were useless. The nurse said that four male nurses tried to restrain her, but they could not overpower her because she was so strong, and they did not want to hurt her. Mom also threatened them with physical violence, and she seemed like she could back it up. The nurse asked if I would be willing to come to the API and talk to Mom to try to get her to settle down. They had called Farrah, but she had refused because Mom would just attack her again. I said that I would love to come there, so I got some clothes on and went to the API. The nurse was waiting for me in the downstairs lobby. She escorted me deep inside the mental ward where they had Mom in an isolation room. She didn't look like herself as when we dropped her off, but her presence did not scare me at all. She was without makeup, her hair was messed up, and her mouth and lips were extremely dry. I approached her, and her eyes got so big and appeared to fill with joy. The first words out of her mouth were, "Hello, dear." Her voice was a little hoarse. I had seen and heard Mom like that before, so I was all right. I then spoke to Mom in a very humble tone and said, "Hello, Ma, how are you doing?"

She said, "These people are trying to hurt me and give me some poison."

"Mom, they are not trying to hurt you. They only want to help you. They truly care for you, so can you please allow them to do their job so you can get well and get out of here? We miss you at home. Mom, you know I love you very much, and I wouldn't let these good people hurt you. Remember, we talked about Velvet and Ross? And that we were working on a plan to bring them here to be with you, right? You have to get well for them, and me too, but mostly for them because they will need you."

Mom adjusted her body language and immediately humbled herself and said, "You're right, son, I have to get well and be strong for them, Velvet and Ross." Mom was talking like she was a little girl and repeatedly said, "Velvet and Ross, Velvet and Ross, Velvet and Ross."

I then said to Mom, "Will you please take the medicine these nurses have for you so you can get better?"

"Yes, son. You are such a dear son to your mother." I motioned to the nurses, and they brought over the medication. Mom took the medicine and swallowed it. Mom immediately wanted to lay down, so the nurses asked her to go with them, and she did. I spoke to Mom as she walked away and said, "Mom, I will come back to see you tomorrow and see how you are doing."

"Thank you, my dear son. I will be fine, and I love you, son." Mom always spoke with deep expression when she said "son" to me. When Mom spoke, she truly meant every statement and ended it with "son." That truly made me feel special, and I knew then that Mom was very serious about what she was going to do, and that was to get well for all her kids, especially for Velvet and Ross. Mom then walked out of the isolation room and disappeared through some doors with several nurses. I felt completely at peace, and I went home. The next morning, I called the API and spoke with a nurse, and she said that Mom was sleeping very soundly and peacefully. I did not want to disturb her, so I told the nurse to call me if they needed anything. The nurse thanked me for all my help in getting Mom to settle down and said goodbye. A few days passed, and the phone rang, and the caller ID read that it was an incoming call from the API. It was Mom. She spoke very calmly and like she was at ease with herself, but her voice was still a little hoarse and sounded dry. She said, "Hello, son, how are you?"

I said, "I am fine. Mom, you sound really good."

She said, "My voice is hoarse, but I am fine. Son, can you and Farrah bring me some clothes, some undergarments, my makeup, and my wig?"

Back then, Mom wore a lot of different types of wigs. I said, "Sure. We will bring it as soon as we can."

"Thank you, son. Bye."

I then called Farrah and told her what Mom wanted, and we retrieved those items and took them to her. Mom would be in the API for about a month, and we would go visit her just about every other day. During the visits, Mom would accept Farrah, but I could tell that Farrah's attempts to be kind to her still made her frustrated. Even though Farrah was almost twenty years old, she still acted as if she was a little girl around Mom, and I think that irritated Mom as well. Mom would tell me she loved being in the hospital because people cared for her and she loved the food. Mom loved being served, and it made her feel like a queen. I had lunch with her a couple of times, and I loved the food as well. I guess that was where I got that acquired taste, because from that point on, I would always love hospital food. It reminded me of Mom and those challenging times. Hospital food made things seem even more right and healthy, and it meant that healing was taking place. The time Mom and I shared together were great times.

Mom eventually got out of the API, and all we talked about was sending for Velvet and Ross. When we were all a family in one house, Mom used to call Velvet "Bug." Bug was a loving description of Velvet probably because Mom loved ladybugs, and since Velvet was a little girl, she took off the lady and called her "bug." A bug was a beautiful, innocent creature to Mom, which was adorable. As we were making plans to send for Velvet and Ross, she would say with such excitement, "Velvet, my bug," with a big smile on her face. Getting those two back was a great motivator for Mom to get well and stay well.

CHAPTER EIGHT

We kidnap my sister Velvet and steal my brother Ross and bring them to Anchorage, Alaska; Mom has one last nervous breakdown

It was around June 1982, and Mom was finally out of the hospital. Mom was looking good and feeling good, but she wasn't 100 percent happy because her two babies were still in other states. Velvet was in Long Branch, California, and Ross was somewhere close to Walter, Texas. When I left Dad's house in Fort Gold in 1980, Tiffany, Farrah, and Farrah's big brown teddy bear left with me, and we drove Tiffany to go live with her mother in Port Agnes, Texas. But that adventure would be a disaster in itself, and the decision to drive Tiffany to live with her mother is one I wish I would have thought more thoroughly about. That decision was the turning point that altered my life forever. When I made that decision to take Tiffany to find and live with her mother because she was running from her father, that was the ultimate reason why I left Dad's house in Fort Gold.

Tiffany's father was a captain in the army, and he had full legal custody of her, and he wasn't having it. We found out that Tiffany was pregnant, and at the time, I thought it was me who got her pregnant, but years later she would tell me that it was really by another boy named Josh Godwin. One day, in the heat of an argument, we were talking about her pregnancy, and Tiffany told me she was not pregnant with my child but with Josh Godwin's. And now that I think about it many years later and juggle that situation in my mind, I realize that was probably why Tiffany couldn't go through with the abortion, knowing that she was going to destroy another boy's baby and she hadn't even told him she was pregnant with his kid. Tiffany told her dad that she was pregnant, and he ordered her to get an abortion. Tiffany's dad demanded that I take her to Austin, Texas, to get the abortion done there. We made it to the doctor's office, and Tiffany walked into the office by herself. I stayed in the car while she had the procedure done, and after about an hour, Tiffany walked back out to the car and told me she was too afraid to get the abortion done. I tried to talk her into getting it done, but she refused, so we ended up leaving and driving back home. I dropped her off at her house. Tiffany walked into the house and told her dad she couldn't go through with the abortion, and he was furious. He made a few calls to Dallas, Texas, and he ended up taking her there and getting the abortion done. After they returned home, he demanded that Tiffany not see me anymore, but she refused and ended up running away to my house, where I was still staying with Dad in Fort Gold. Tiffany's dad did not like that and started searching for her and telling people that he was going to put her in a girl's home, but I couldn't let that happen, so I took it upon myself to drive her to her mother who was living in Port Agnes, Texas.

I left behind a great job at Western Sizzlin' with a great store manager named C. L. Scott, but more important than my job, that move caused me and Farrah to leave behind our youngest brother Ross, who was fourteen, and the baby of the family, Velvet, who was eleven. Dad was depending on me and Farrah to help him care for Ross and Velvet. Farrah and I ended up not going back at all to Fort Gold. That was not our plan, but it just happened that way. Had we known of the severity of our decision, we probably would have returned because when Farrah and I did not come back, Dad decided to send Velvet and Ross to places where they could be well taken care of. Dad had to do it because he received orders to go back to Korea to complete his duty that was interrupted when he was called back because Mom had a nervous breakdown. I feel like Dad wanted to go back to Korea to either regain some rank that he had lost or to receive some extra rank to get ahead, which he needed if he wanted to retire at a higher pay scale. Dad had to do something with Ross and Velvet, so he made a major decision to fly Velvet to Long Branch, California, to live with his sister Isabell Rock, and he sent Ross to an unknown lady near Whisper, Texas. Why Dad decided against sending Velvet and Ross to Mom in Alaska, we had no idea. He either thought Mom was not stable enough, or he didn't want to give up his parental and custodial rights.

In the meantime, we started working on our plan to steal Ross and kidnap Velvet. Ross was the easier sibling to get to, so we put our focus on him first. Ross first contacted us, but he had no idea where he was. We asked him to look around and ask others to find out where he was without being suspicious or alerting the people he was staying with. Ross would go to a pay phone and call us, and we stayed in touch quite regularly. Eventually, he found out where he was and told us he was in a town near Whisper, Texas. We couldn't believe that Dad would send him there with people we didn't know. At first, we couldn't believe that he was close to a town near Whisper, far from our own relatives with whom he could have stayed. Then that disbelief turned into a blessing because Farrah's boyfriend Roger was from Whisper. What a darn coincidence. Immediately, we contacted Roger's family and told them of our dilemma, and they were extremely glad to assist. They even located the house where Ross was staying, but they stayed away. By then, we had already saved up enough money for Ross's one-way ticket. At that time, if my memory serves me correctly, the ticket only cost a little under $400. The ticket we purchased would be waiting at the ticket counter at the airport for Ross to retrieve. Well, the time had come to put our plan into action. We told Ross to leave at a specified time and to wait at a certain area that Roger's family had designated as a rendezvous spot. Ross went to that spot, which was some bushes as was described to us, and he was picked up and taken to the airport. Roger's family member said they put Ross on the plane, and all we had to do was wait. The flight would take twelve hours, so we went to our own homes and rested. Mom could hardly contain herself, but she was good because she knew she had to be in good condition to take care of Ross. Well, it was time to go to the airport to pick him up, and back in

1983, you could go deep into the airport to the hangar exits and wait for your family member to step off the plane. We looked at the arrival board, and it said that Ross's plane had arrived on time. People started walking off the plane, and I, Farrah, and Roger could hardly contain ourselves. We looked at Mom and saw extreme excitement in her eyes and in her body language. Mom started crying, and then suddenly, there he was. It was Ross, and he looked well. We all hugged Ross and cried at the same time. It was mass hysteria, and we almost couldn't believe we had achieved such a feat. We had grown up. We went home to Mom's place to celebrate and talked almost all night.

Such a relief we had, but it wasn't over because we quickly had to shift our energy and focus into getting Velvet. We didn't inform Dad right away because we didn't want to alert him and have his sister Isabell put clamps on Velvet. Now the real work was to begin because we had to quickly devise a plan to get Velvet. She stayed in touch with us on a regular basis simply because she was with Dad's sister Isabell. We asked Velvet if she knew anyone she could trust to get her to the airport, and she did have someone. Velvet's ticket would cost more than Ross's, I would say close to $500, and it was a round-trip ticket because that was the cheapest we could get, but we knew she would not be going back. The time was early 1983, and we were ready to put our plan into action. Velvet had a much farther car ride to the airport from Long Branch to Los Angeles. The risk was high that Dad had found out what happened to Ross, so we were extremely relieved after we got confirmation from Velvet's friend that she was taken to the airport and got onto the plane. The flight from Los Angeles to Anchorage would be about five hours compared to Ross's twelve hours. Now the time had come to head to the airport, and it was extremely cold that evening. We did not know how Velvet was going to take the cold, but we were prepared because Mom had already gotten her a winter coat and snow boots. We arrived at the airport and walked into the area where Velvet's plane was to taxi. We looked up at the arrival board, and it said that Velvet's plane had arrived on time. People started exiting the plane, and it seemed that Velvet was taking forever, but because she was an eleven-year-old girl, she had to be one of the last to exit the plane because she had to be escorted by a flight attendant. And then right before our eyes there she was, our baby sister. She looked a little different since the last time Farrah and I saw her back in Fort Gold because by now, it had been almost three years, but she appeared to be healthy. Mom just melted with happiness and gratefulness and hugged her baby, her Bug, for what seemed like eternity. We were all extremely relieved and full of joy. We waited only one day to tell Dad that Velvet was with us because we didn't want him to worry. Now four of Mom's children were with her, and she was extremely happy, but one was still missing. The order in which Mom's kids made it to Alaska to be with her is as follows: Farrah made it in 1980, I made it in 1981, Ross made it in 1982, and Velvet made it in 1983. Only Wayne was not with us, but he would eventually come to Alaska in the later part of 1983. The whole ordeal seemed like God ordered it that way, and we were all so blessed after that because Mom wouldn't have a nervous breakdown or mental illness relapse and wouldn't have to go to the API again for twenty years. But once that twenty-year hiatus had come and gone, Mom's sickness would catch us off guard, change our lives again, and would puzzle us until her death.

CHAPTER NINE

Mom's mental illness awakens after a twenty-one-year
hiatus; Farrah's behavior is questionable; I am involved
in five life-threatening incidents in one year

A manda Jean Rock-Vance-Jones would be well for twenty years.
She would have small glimpses of her sickness, but for the
most part, she would not have to go to the hospital. Mom
would get the flu and the common cold, and that would be about
it. We believed Mom didn't have a nervous breakdown because of
several definitive reasons. The first reason was the prophetic speaking
by Mom's aunt Scarlet Dodge in 1977, when she said that Mom would
not get sick anymore if she moved to Alaska; second was the return of
Mom's five children to her; third was Mom's willingness to be successful
in every aspect of her life; and fourth were the direct blessings from
God Almighty himself. I know that God had always watched over my
mother, and he did so without giving her everything she wanted. God
always gave Mom everything she needed and gave her a few of her
wants. Mom used to tell me a favorite quote of hers, which was, "God
gives you all your needs and some of your wants." And that was what
God did for her. Mom was so determined to stay well that she went
out and found a job. I went to go see her on her job. The very first job
she got was at an establishment, a Burger King located on the corner
of Northern Richmond Boulevard and Beaver Parkway. Mom was very

proud of her job, but she was not happy because she was on her feet a lot, and she had to bend over a lot because she was the custodian there. The hours weren't long, and the pay was very little, but she was willing to do it so she could care for Ross and Velvet better. Mom did her best to give them everything they needed, but the job at Burger King would not last long because God had something better in store for her, so she quit. Mom struggled finding a good doctor that would monitor her condition and behavior, but she eventually found one that she simply loved, and he was Dr. Detrick Samuelson Sr. He would be Mom's doctor for twenty years, and under his medical care, Mom would prosper and live a successful life on her own. Mom also befriended a lady named Mia. I do not know her last name, but she and Mom were inseparable for about three to four years. They would meet at their main spot at a Village Inn restaurant two or three times a week to sit and drink coffee and grab an occasional meal. The friendship helped Mom remain stable, and I believe it was good therapy for Mia as well because they both had been hospitalized for mental issues.

It was around 1987, and Velvet was around eighteen years old and still living with Mom. She was wearing Mom's patience thin because Velvet would stay out late a lot just like teenagers do, but that didn't work for Mom because she would be up late worried about her. One day they got into an argument, and it was decided that Velvet needed to move out. Even though she had moved out, Mom still worried about her. Mom's great friend Mia became ill and soon passed away. It was devastating for Mom. Mom's medication made her sleep a lot, and Mia's passing had her sleeping a lot more because she was extremely sad. I believe Mia knew she was not going to live much longer, so before she died, Mom bought Mia's car from her. It was a green 1975 Oldsmobile Cutlass, and she really loved that car. Mom kept a lot of her belongings in that car, including her church stuff and Bible. One day, Mom was letting it warm up, idling in her car spot like usual, and it caught fire and burned up. The fire department arrived and put the fire out, but the car was ruined. Mom was left without a vehicle for a little while until she purchased her very own 1985 Cadillac Eldorado. It was two-tone brown and beige, and she loved that car. Mom felt important, like she was a queen. She had accomplished some things on her own, and that made her very proud. Mom moved from the apartment where Mia's car burned up, and she and Ross rented an apartment on Turnpike Street. At that downstairs apartment, Mom found herself a handsome white boyfriend named Tom. Mom told me that for a little over a year, she and Tom slept together in the same bed but never had sex, and that is all I know about their relationship. At that apartment, Ross also found his future bride, Maria Gonzalez. One other unique thing that happened for Mom at that apartment was that she befriended a young moose. The moose would come to her kitchen window and stick its head in almost every day at the same time, and Mom would feed it. She would pet it and talk to it, and the young moose never became aggressive. There were quite a few things that helped in Mom's stability, and it was a blessing. I can't leave out Mother's church that she loved dearly. She was a member of Ezekiel Missionary Baptist Church for almost forty years until she passed, and the pastor was Rev. Dr. A. B. Mayweather.

Mom's uncle Damon Jones also lived in Alaska in the city of Fairfax, and he was the brother to Scarlet Dodge. Damon loved my mother very dearly. We called him Uncle Dom. He had a daughter living in Anchorage, and her name was Tori Howard, but we called her Teepee. She was engaged to a man name Big Chris Maddox aka Big C, and he loved himself some Teepee. He was the head postmaster in human resources at the main post office in Anchorage. He also loved and cared for my mother. Teepee talked to Big C and asked him if he could help and get Mom a job with the post office. Big C said he would see if there was something he could do, and he told Mom to apply for a job with the post office. He helped her with the application process, and she passed the required qualifications and was eventually hired at the post office. I am not exactly sure what her job description was, but I believe she was performing the duties of a building plant operator. Mom worked the graveyard shift starting at eleven o'clock in the evening and ending at seven o'clock in the morning. I would visit her quite often, and she would be so glad that I would visit her. Mom loved her job at the post office, and Big C took very good care of her there. Mom would work for the post office for over fifteen years. Mom would move from apartment to apartment to duplex and eventually end up in a one-bedroom apartment that she would live in for twenty years. The apartment was in the low-income housing area located on Gettysburg Hill, and she simply loved that one-bedroom apartment. After Mom was on the job at the post office for about sixteen years, Big C would eventually be forced to retire because of health reasons. He was Mom's protector and overseer and didn't let anybody mess with her. Soon, Mom would get a new supervisor, and he would give her a hard time and eventually force her into early retirement.

Mom's mental state and condition was so good that we had family gatherings often, and they were held mostly at Farrah's house. We would sing together and even record one another on cassette tape singing and laughing and just having great times. But there were some problems in between those times, and it was not Mom this time, it was Farrah. Her behavior should have been called into question, but because of the things we had dealt with Mom, Farrah's behaviors and antics appeared somewhat normal. After Roger and Farrah moved away from the apartment complex where she had stabbed Roger, they moved across the street to a duplex on Lakeview Circle Drive. The first incident that happened at that duplex shocked me beyond belief. One day, I was called by Farrah to come over to her house because she was concerned about her son Trey, and for some reason, I knew it was not going to be good. I drove over to the duplex that she and Roger shared and walked through the front door. It looked like a tornado had gone through the place. The glass coffee table was broken into little pieces, the couch had been shredded, the microwave had been used as a projectile weapon, dirt was everywhere from several plants that had been thrown throughout the place, and the top part of the commode that covered the water basin of the toilet was broken in half. Farrah told me that while they were fighting and throwing stuff at each other, their son, who was less than a year old, was on the floor right in the middle of them. Roger went and picked Mom up and brought her over to their house probably to have her help calm Farrah down, but they remained in the car talking, probably trying to come up with a plan on how to deal with her. The car was parked on the street in front of the house, and Mom was sitting in the passenger's seat while Roger was sitting behind the wheel. In the meantime, Farrah was in the house pacing and still fuming with anger at Roger because she was the type of person to not let things go. She always wanted to get the last word in, and apparently she decided that she was not done with getting back at Roger, so she went outside, found an iron pickax that didn't have a wooden handle, and ran toward the car. She approached the side of the car that Mom was sitting in and got right up the door. She hurled the pickax right through the window in an attempt to hit Roger. The window was shattered and just narrowly missed Mom's head. Mom looked at Farrah in disbelief. The pickax landed right in the middle of Roger and Mom, not hurting either one of them. The police were not called in that incident, probably because they didn't want neither one to go to jail. The dirt, glass, trash, uprooted plants from the fight remained on the floor throughout the house for over two weeks because both refused to clean it up. They just walked over the mess like it was part of their décor.

Farrah and Roger would have several more fight like that one, and all of them would be just as intense. Because Farrah and Roger fought so often, they were forced to move from the Lakeview Circle address several miles away to a duplex on Rigger Street. At that address I would see the aftermath of a ten-pound round workout weight that had been hurled through the air, shattering the screen of a large color console and being lodged in it for about a week for any visitors to see. They both took things to the extreme. In the twenty years that Mom was mentally stable and healthy, Ross, Velvet, and Wayne would leave Alaska and never return, not even to visit their own mother. That should tell you readers that they were ashamed of our mother and her condition, or just cared about themselves. How do you not visit your very own mother where she has lived for over thirty years? Wayne was the only one to come visit Mom for the first time since leaving some fifteen years earlier, but it was not a good visit because Wayne came without giving us a warning or notice. And because Mom did not receive prior notification, she would not let Wayne into her apartment. You will understand why as you continue reading, and I will just say that Mom didn't want Wayne going back telling her business.

Like I was saying, in the twenty years that Mom was mentally stable and healthy, I would divorce and marry again and see my side of some close calls with death in 1997. At that time, I had been working in the Strategic air defense as a defense clerk II for nine years. God blessed me, and I started that job on September 2, 1988. It was March 21, 1997, a Friday, and I would leave my job on time just like I had done so many times before. On my drive home, about a quarter of a mile away from my home, I drove past a mom-and-pop store that was on my left side, and I prepared to turn on my right turn signal so I could turn right when suddenly, my left arm slowly started curling up toward my chest. Keep in mind that my 1984 Chevy Camaro was still in motion. I looked down at my arm in shock, and I couldn't stop it from curling up toward my chest. The only thing I thought that may have been happening to me was that I must be having a heart attack—my mom would tell me that if a person was to feel pain and weakness in their left arm, they might be having a heart attack. I was saying to myself that if I was having a heart attack and died at the wheel, the car would probably speed down the road and kill people, and I did not want that for my family to deal with. Let me inform you that I was thinking in milliseconds, so I decided to just shift/jam the car into park without stopping as soon as I could, and I did. My left arm continued to curl up toward my chest, and once again I was thinking in milliseconds. I decided to call on the name of Jesus Christ as loudly as I could, and right after I said those words, I blanked out. That whole incident happened in less than a minute. The next thing I remember is waking up in the back of an ambulance with paramedics looking down over me. I asked them what happened, and they said that it looked like I had a seizure and that I was lucky to be alive. They said some people at the mom-and-pop store saw my car idling in the middle of the street, came over, and saw me inside having a seizure. They broke the window, unlocked the door, and pulled me out right before the car caught fire. The car caught fire because I did not turn the car off after I shifted/ jammed it into park, and while having the seizure, my foot was on the gas pedal revving up the engine to its highest RPMs for minutes. The engine overheated and subsequently burst into flames. The people pulled me out just before the car was completely engulfed in flames. At some point while having the seizure, I bit my tongue and pissed myself. I spent two days in the hospital, and the doctor had no idea what caused me to have that seizure because I had never had one before in my life. The doctor also concluded that I had a grand mal seizure because I had the seizure for almost an hour, as per eyewitnesses at the scene. The doctor prescribed me some anti-seizure medication and told me I could not drive for six months, but I never took the medication, and to this day I have not had another seizure. When I went home after two days in the hospital, the car was towed to my front yard, completely burnt up and destroyed.

I got well and became healthy again. Two months passed by, and the day was May 21, 1997. I purchased a speed bike from a garage sale because I wanted to ride a much faster bike, plus I wanted to keep up with my friend Elmore Spaulding, who rode a speed bike. I wanted to be able to ride together with him, and I couldn't because the bikes I owned were either mountain or trail bikes, and Elmore had long legs and could ride really fast. I took off on this speed bike to go to my friend's house that was about five miles away, and I got about halfway to my destination. I approached an intersection where the church I attended regularly was on my right. By now I was going downhill on a sidewalk, traveling at a very high speed—more than I was used too. As I got closer to this "T" intersection by the church, I saw that the sidewalk kind of winded and curved a little bit. I was not able to maneuver the bike very well because I was going so fast. I barely crossed the "T" intersection under control, and I made it over to the other side of the sidewalk, but right after that, I lost control of the bike, and it slammed into a large metal light pole. I just narrowly missed hitting the pole head-on, but I did slam my left shoulder into the pole. When the bike hit the pole, I was catapulted forward about fifteen feet into the ditch. Luckily for me, a police officer was driving by at the same time and turned around and helped me. I was disoriented for about a minute, and the police officer shook me and asked if I was okay. I asked him to drive me to my friend's, where I was going. I only bruised my shoulder, and I would eventually be okay. What a coincidence, because just before that accident, I had heard on the news that Sonny Bono was skiing when he slammed into a tree, hitting it head-on and dying from his injuries. After I got home, I thought to myself that it was exactly two months from the day that I had the seizure accident. I said to myself that God was really looking over me because that biking accident happened right in front of the church I attended.

And you are not going to believe this, but a third incident happened to me on July 21, 1997. I would yet again have a close call with death. Me and my friend Vincent Otto made plans to go fishing for a few days to a popular fish camp site called Blue Water Creek. At that time of the year, many different species of salmon, especially king salmon, came in far from the ocean depths to spawn in the fresh water streams. When the salmon came in, the halibut also came in to more shallow waters to feed off the salmon carcass that flowed back down stream in the confluence of the ocean after they die from spawning. They also fed off the skeletal remains after the salmon had been filleted by the many fishermen. Well on July 21, Vincent and I jumped into my twelve-foot Zodiac boat and motored out to my popular spot. First, we trolled for king salmon, and both of us caught one. After that, we boated out a little farther and then anchored down and started fishing for halibut. Normally when we caught fish, we just put them inside the boat, but this knucklehead time I decided to put my fish on a rope stringer and have them hang off the back of the stern tied to my twenty-five-horsepower motor to keep them fresh in the water. By now I had one king salmon and one twenty-pound halibut on my stringer. When fishing for halibut, you are fishing from the bottom of the ocean, and as I was waiting patiently, suddenly the water turned really still, like it was slack tide. The water looked like glass, and it got extremely quiet, almost like you could hear a pebble drop in the water. I looked down at my stringer, and it was no longer waving in the water but hanging straight down. I then heard a swooshing sound that made me think whales were in the area, so I looked for them, but I didn't see any. I then turned back to look down at my stringer, and immediately I was surprised beyond belief. My eyes almost popped out of my head when I saw this stellar giant sea lion slowly coming up with its large finlike hands reaching for my fish. I immediately grabbed the stringer and pulled the fish out of the water and into the boat, but I didn't pull them all the way in, leaving the one large fin of the halibut still hanging over the stern. The sea lion had his eyes fixed on that tail and kept coming for it. The sea lion was about three or four feet away from my motor, and I quickly pulled the fin completely into the boat and used my fishing pole to hit the water to scare the sea lion, and it stopped moving. The sea lion just waded in the water and stared at me with this hungry. angry look on its face for a few seconds and then descended into the depths of the water. As a precaution, I took out my .38 special and shot into the water to scare it some more. Then my friend Vincent screamed and said the sea lion was in front of the boat, but it quickly swam off. We were both so terrified that we decided to pull the anchor up and get off the water and motor to shore. That fright couldn't escape me. I kept thinking that had that sea lion grabbed a hold of my fish stringer, it would have no doubt flipped the boat and put is in the freezing water, since the stringer was tied to the stern where the motor was. I never tied a stringer to the stern again. My Zodiac was twelve-feet-long, and that sea lion was twice the size of my boat.

I know you are probably thinking there can't be another accident or incident, but you are wrong. On September 21, 1997, two months later, something else would happen to me. Because I had a blended family, my wife at the time wanted me to get rid of my daughter who she thought was a terrible kid; she wanted me to send her to her crackhead mother living in Dallas, Texas. I refused that demand because I had already sent my other daughter to her crackhead mother, so my wife at the time decided to move out of the house we shared. This was on September 21, 1997. Her leaving me did hurt but was not that painful, and I soon moved forward in my life—or at least I thought. After just two months, would you believe, my wife wanted to come back home, but I strongly refused and put up as much fight as I could until one day, on November 21, 1997, two months since my last test, if I can say. I got off work, drove home, and pulled into my driveway. I couldn't believe my eyes. Someone had smeared large amounts of olive oil all over the front and back of the house and on the door handles. I assumed my wife's girlfriends came over to the house while I was at work and smeared the olive oil on the house to get the spirit of God to move me to change my mind and let her back into the house. After a tactic like that, I gave in and let her back into the house. It was the worst mistake I could have made. She sexed me up after I let her back in, and then she turned into Ms. She-devil. We would divorce six years later. That year was a test of all sorts for some reason, and I guess I passed the test by the skin of my teeth because I am still alive to tell the story. If God was testing me, I am still waiting on my reward for passing. I finished the year of 1997, sighed with relief, and looked back and wondered what happened and why it happened to me and why I survived.

CHAPTER TEN

The twenty-three-year mental stability ends,
and Mom's condition worsens; we enter her
apartment for the first time in ten years

T he last time Mom had a serious setback in her mental illness was in early 1982. The time now was 2005, and Mom suffered her first major nervous breakdown/mental illness relapse in twenty-three years. I started writing this book in 2014, and for medical terminology from a doctor's diagnosis, I now call Mom's condition as bipolar disorder. But as I edit, I am forced to change Mom's known condition again because I have found more concrete evidence detailing her condition, and the name of it is paranoid personality disorder. Mom's personal doctor diagnosed her as having bipolar disorder, but her condition was that and much more. Over the course of twenty-three years, we would see glimpses of her bipolar disorder, but never full-scale incidents. Somehow Mom knew how to control her episodes, and she was very good with it. Farrah and I wondered how she did it, but we didn't put too much effort into finding out because it was working, and we didn't want to mess up a good thing by prying into her business too much. Mom knew how to function with her condition—and function quite successfully at that. She was completely normal in every way if she took her medication on time and correctly. Whatever she was doing was working very well for her. But after twenty-three years, Mom had a full-blown relapse, and we were forced to admit her into the API, the Alaska Psychiatric Institute. At that time in 2005, we were puzzled and outright confused, but we weren't alarmed just yet. Naturally Farrah and I involved the whole family, and we did so under the advice of our father. Farrah and I first sought out Dad's advice because of his experience in years of dealing with Mom. He thought it was best that all the siblings be involved and take an active role in helping Mom, and so everyone did. The most helpful out of all the siblings was Velvet. She would make many calls to Mom from her Dallas home, talking to her, keeping her calm, and finding out her whereabouts physically and mentally. Wayne was so concerned that he flew to Alaska to see about her, but his visit was not a pleasant one because he came unannounced. Farrah and I were not prepared for his visit, and Mom even less so. Wayne did not stay long, maybe three or four days, because he needed to return to Texas for his job. By now I was living close to Mom on Gettysburg Hill in the Prospect View Apartments. Going through a divorce put me in a good position to get a place close to Mom, and it was a relief for me knowing I was so close to her. I used to go talk to the managers of the Prospect View Apartments just in case they needed help with Mom. I used to go talk to them long before I moved there. The first manager I used to talk to was a man, and the second manager was a lady. I believe it was a relief for them knowing that I lived so close to Mom because she could be a handful at times. Her standards were high, and it appeared that the management had reached their limits and patience with her. Mom would pay her rent late on a regular basis over the course of twenty years, but even more so once she had retired so that she could make ends meet. She needed to do that because she was on a shoestring budget. Mom had a taste for luxurious items. She would shop at Nordstrom on a regular basis. The first car Mom purchased on her own was a beautiful Cadillac Eldorado, and she was stylish in it. With me living so close to her, I could keep close tabs on her, and I believe Mom felt a little at ease knowing I was right across the hall in another building from her.

Now Mom would have to be put in the API two more times within a six-month period, and the entire family was starting to get really concerned. We were scratching our heads wondering what could have gone so wrong after all these years for Mom to be put in the API in back-to-back instances. Our regular routine for getting Mom in the API went like this: we first noticed signs of change, like her eye color almost glazing over or her becoming very suspicious of everyone and not trusting them, especially Farrah. Or we would hear her talking to herself. The real big notification was something all too familiar: she would call certain family members in the lower 48 states to Texas. I used to get calls from my cousin Fiona Branch saying that Mom was calling her and not sounding right. Once Farrah or I knew those signs were at a concerning level, we would check on Mom, but when we did, she would not let us into her apartment. Mom had not let us into her apartment for ten years now.

I know it sounds hard to believe, but none of us had been in her apartment for at least ten years or more. Now you will not believe this, but Velvet had sent for Mom to visit her in Texas, and while she was gone, Mom allowed an unknown stranger to check on her apartment while she was gone. Mom refused to tell us who that person was. While Mom was gone to Texas, I saw someone driving her car, which was a small white four-door Oldsmobile sedan. I first had to make sure it was Mom's car, and it was, because Mom had a lot of papers and books in the back window. I was shocked and immediately assumed someone had stolen it, so I followed it to a very small house. I saw a short young oriental lady get out of the car and into a house. I called the police and reported the car stolen. A few moments later, a police officer met me at the house, and then we went to the front door and knocked on it. The small oriental lady answered the door. I asked her what she was doing driving my mother's car, and she replied, "Ms. Amanda let me drive her car while she was out of town, and she also asked me to watch her house and water her plants." I was shocked again. I told the young lady that I was Ms. Amanda's son, and I apologized to her and the officer before I left. I immediately called Farrah and told her what happened, and she was shocked as well.

Now let me get back to Mom's apartment. None of Mom's children had been in her apartment for at least ten years because she never invited us there, so after the third time of Mom being put into the API in a span of ten months, Farrah and I were able to get a copy of the key to her apartment from the landlord. The landlord was not supposed to give us a copy of the key, but she did so out of desperation to help Mom and for the safety of the other tenants. When I stepped into Mom's apartment, I was in a state of utter shock. I could not believe my eyes. Mom's apartment had a small kitchen with a very small bathroom, a small living room area, and one bedroom for a total of 522 square feet of living space. It was about the size of a small classroom, and I could barely enter through the front door because she had clothes hanging off the closet door next to the front door, and the closet itself was overflowing with clothes as well. I was only able to open the front door about two feet to get in, and once I got in, I was in total shock. I was in awe. The inside of her apartment was almost indescribable and indistinguishable from the last time I was in there. The living room had hat and shoe boxes that stood three feet high and took up three quarters of the living room space, and all the boxes had hats and shoes in them. From where I was standing, I could see the bathroom, so I walked to it, and it was incredible. Clothes had taken up most of the space on the shower curtain bar. And there were lots of makeup items all over the bathroom. As I stood just outside the entryway of the bathroom, I could see directly into Mom's bedroom, and it was a sight to see. Mom's bed was right in front of me, and the right side of the bed had clothes stacked two feet high. That side of the bed had not been slept on in years by my count, and the left side of the bed was empty, but I could see the mattress. The light burgundy mattress was very expensive, but the top cushion part of the mattress was completely worn out. About a 3x1-foot section was missing because of the firm cotton being carried away by attaching itself to her clothing. In other words, Mom had only slept on the left side of her bed for many years. The bed she had was expensive because I paid for it with my credit card, and Mom paid me back every penny and then some. Her bedroom closet was completely packed, and she had clothes hanging from the closet door and on her dresser drawers. There were all types of jewelry and merchandise on her bedroom floor and on her dresser. There were also clothes, shoes, and small gifts on the bedroom floor.

I left her bedroom thinking that I was finished in being shocked, but I wasn't. As I approached the kitchen, I started smelling mildew and wretchedness. I got to the edge of the kitchen thinking I had seen enough clothes hanging all over the place, but there were rows and rows of clothes hanging from the kitchen cabinet doors. There were about five large bags of garbage in the corner of the kitchen, and it stank. My brother Wayne purchased Mom a small 3.5-cubic-foot upright freezer over twenty years ago, long before she moved into that apartment, and it appeared to me that it had not worked for years—or shall I say it was devoid of any Freon to freeze food, but it was still plugged into the outlet. It was still running because I could hear it, and it still had food in it, but it was mildewed five times over and stank like a city dump site. The next task I needed to consider was to look in the refrigerator. I was afraid too, but the curiosity was killing me, so I grabbed the handle and pulled, and I saw the horror. The refrigerator was packed with mildewed food. It was so disgusting to see that I couldn't believe this was the home of my mother. I took a closer look at the sofa, and only the left side of the sofa had been sat on for many years from my estimate. A hole had formed because the springs had broken, and the cushion was completely worn out. There were three additional pillows in place of the worn-out surface. I stopped in my footsteps and began to cry.

I called my sister Farrah to tell her the condition of Mom's apartment, and she couldn't believe it. Farrah didn't come with me this first time because she was afraid Mom would come back and find her there. Even though we knew Mom was in a locked facility for at least a month, we both still did not feel good about being in her place, truly believing she might walk in there at any moment. It was terrifying. I told Farrah that I must videotape this apartment and send it to the *Olivia Wild Show* to see if Olivia and her producers could help us with Mom and her condition. I left the apartment and did not move anything out of place other than taking out the trash. Farrah and I could now relax knowing that Mom was in the API getting the help she needed. The next day, Farrah and I tried to take her some clothes and health care items, but they wouldn't let us see her for the first seventy-two hours of being placed there. Well I went back a week later, and they allowed me to see her, but now they had moved her to the new building, which was an even more secure facility. I went in and spoke to her for a little bit, and she was doing quite well. She asked me to get with Farrah and get some clothes, makeup, and other items for her, and she suggested that I come back in the morning and have breakfast with her. The very next morning, I got up early and went and had breakfast with her. When I saw Mom, she looked like she was on cloud nine. She was so relaxed and at peace, it was incredible. I used to call her Maw instead of Mom, so I said to her, "Maw, you look really good and happy." Mom said, "Son, I am happy because I like coming to the API because they treat me good, and sometimes I need to rest and relax. I have people around me who I can help, and I like helping people." I said, "That is great, Maw," and we enjoyed a fulfilling, healthy breakfast. I left Mom, but I hated to leave her there because the place was like a fortress, and there was no way of getting out.

Now Farrah and I assumed Mom would be there for at least another two or three weeks, but we were wrong. Only a week passed by since I last saw her, and she was out already. We were shocked. The doctors and workers at the API could not keep her for long periods of time because of new HIPAA laws. HIPAA is an acronym for Health Insurance Portability and Accountability Act, the federal law that protects personal medical information and recognizes the rights to relevant medical information of family caregivers and others directly involved in providing or paying for care. It had been twenty-three years since we were last involved with Mom going to the API, and we were out of touch and had no idea that the laws had been reformed. In the past, we could get all sorts of medical information about Mom and her condition and progress, and we used to have input as to how long to keep her in the API, but the laws had changed to protect Mom, the patient. No longer could someone just be put in a mental institution and stored there for long periods of time. The patient now had rights that far exceeded the concern of their family members. Farrah and I tried to get information on her condition and whereabouts, but the API personnel and doctors had no obligation to tell us anything, and we were her damn kids who carried the burden of overseeing her and her well-being. I found out that Mom was at her apartment, and I was biting my fingernails because Mom was settling in. I was afraid of what she was going to say to me, but I was stunned when I called her on the phone. She complimented me on taking out her trash. She really appreciated it. Mom's safe haven was her home, and things were back to normal—or so we thought.

Six months passed, and she was acting out of character again, and now the whole family was really concerned. Mom's condition got so bad that we had to put her into the API again. All of us kids were struggling to find some answers, so we decided to find Mom's doctor. Dr. Samuelson was Mom's doctor who had treated her for over twenty years, and if anybody knew what was going on with her, it would be him. We located his office, and when we set up an appointment to talk to him, we were hit with a major Joe Frazier blow. We found Dr. Samuelson all right, but it was not the Dr. Samuelson we were looking for. It was Dr. Detrick Samuelson Jr, not Dr. Detrick Samuelson Sr., who had retired. I went in to talk to him, and there was only so much he could tell because of the HIPAA laws, but before we left, he did tell me that he and Mom did not get along. I left Dr. Samuelson Jr.'s office scratching my head and went to go talk to Mom. She said she hated the son so much that she was not willing to compromise and use his services at all, and because she refused to cooperate with Dr. Samuelson Jr., he had to terminate his service with Mom. So now we found out what the problem was. That stability that Mom had all those twenty-plus years played no role in keeping her well anymore. Mom had a great relationship with Dr. Samuelson Sr. for over twenty years, and the relationship kept her healthy.

We found out that she was now getting her medication from the Alternative Need Health Clinic, and that was exactly what it was, a clinic. A low-level clinic that helped patients with regular, everyday ailments. Mom needed a mental health specialist facility. ANHC was not a mental disorder hospital that helped people with severe mental disabilities, and Mom suffered for it. I was now taking her to see a variety of doctors at ANHC because every appointment was with a different doctor that had to be caught up-to-speed on Mom's health history that was not in her file, and they knew very little about her condition and her history of mental instabilities. The doctors at ANHC would prescribe Mom a limited supply of Band-Aid medication that ran out very quickly. And since Mom was on Medicaid, her benefits would expire on a two or three-month deadline. At the time that I took her, the benefits had expired, and she could no longer get the medication she needed until she scheduled an appointment with the Human and Health Services. I finally asked Mom how she was making it, and she told me that she had been rationing out the medication she received, and majority of the time, she was taking half doses, if any at all, so that the medication could last longer. We finally figured out two major problems as to why she was relapsing so quickly.

The Alaska Psychiatric Institute was a revolving door for Mom. She would be in and out so often that Farrah and I could not keep up. We continued to visit her in the API, but things had really changed as far as Mom's behavior. Mom was more hostile, mean, and physical with us. Farrah and I would take turns getting abused, but Farrah received most of the abuse. I tried extra hard to distract Mom with positive conversations and things that I was doing in my community. To me, Farrah was one of the strongest persons I knew because she endured a lot of abuse from Mom, and it would eventually take its toll on Farrah. Mom's condition took its toll on Farrah well before she became an adult, with Farrah having a dramatic episode of her own as a very little girl, proving to stay consistent with our family history.

Chapter Eleven

Mom is admitted to the Alaska Psychiatric Institute
repeatedly and is evicted from her apartment
where she lived for twenty-three years

The year was 2009, and we are going on our fourth year since Mom started having her relapse. I had moved and lived closer to the main office in the same apartment complex at Prospect View. It had been only a few months since she had been in the API, and the last time was extremely bad, especially for Farrah because Mom really beat her up verbally, and oh my goodness, did Mom say some really mean things to her. As usual, Mom talked about how bad a wife Farrah was to Roger, and she talked about the condition of Farrah's house. The number one thing she talked about was Farrah's weight. Farrah had been quite obese since she had her first child. But the one time that triggered Farrah to fight back was when Mom talked badly about her children. Farrah and Roger took quite a dislike when Mom talked badly about their youngest daughter Sophia. From that point, on Farrah no longer believed Mom had a mental condition 100 percent, and the reason was that Mom appeared to know her surroundings and whereabouts in the midst of her episodes. Mom knew how much money she had on her person. Mom knew exactly when her retirement and disability checks were to arrive. She knew where she lived, and all sorts of familiar things that she related to.

It was June 2009, and Mom was acting a little strange. It was nothing to be really alarmed about, but I was still concerned. I told Farrah and Roger that Mom was acting strange and that she may be off her medication, but Farrah and Roger showed little concern because of the last confrontation. In Mom's last incident, we noticed that she was having conversations with herself, as if someone was in her apartment with her. Farrah and I would go into Mom's building, sneak up to her apartment door, put our ears directly up against the door, and listen. We would hear her hold an ongoing conversation with herself, sometimes in another voice. Farrah and I were confused sometimes because we weren't sure if she was by herself or if she had someone in there with her. She had a neighbor who would stick their hand out of their own apartment and tell us Mom would talk to herself quite often and would get up and slam her entry door quite often. Some days later, I asked Mom why she would slam her door, and she told me that her neighbors would bother her, taunt her, and knock on her door before running back into their apartments, so she would slam her door really hard several times during the day and at night to scare her neighbors to get them to leave her alone. And boy, did her door slam loud and hard. The door appeared to me to be made of solid oak, and it was heavy.

One night in June 2009, I told Farrah that Mom was acting strange and that I thought that we might need to get her into the API. Farrah showed very little concern, so I just went to sleep. Normally I slept very well throughout the night, but as the night went on, I was restless and just tossed and turned, and Mom was very heavy on my mind. At about 3:00 a.m. I was awakened, and I truly believe the Lord woke me up so that I could go check on Mom. I struggled in bed for about twenty minutes, trying to decide if I should go and check on Mom or not. Well my spirit just couldn't rest, so I got up, put some clothes on, and walked across the street to Mom's building, which was about 150 yards away. Thank God I listened to the Lord speaking to me because when I got to Mom's apartment building, I heard her talking very loudly, and then I saw her as I was looking from outside as I approached the building. She was out in the stairwell with a four-foot tree branch, and she was yelling and talking loudly. She had broken a small window in the stairwell. I walked into the building and met Mom at the stairs. Mom couldn't have been there very long because had she been there for a long time, someone would have called the police on her. Once again I thanked God for speaking to my spirit to go over there when I did. My approach was always very humble and with compassion. I said, "Hey Maw, how are you doing, what's going on?" Mom seemed to be surprised by me, and she quickly went into her apartment. As I walked up the stairs, one of the tenants came out and said that Mom had been carrying on like that for a couple of hours, which I doubted, and that she had gotten worse and they had called the police. I looked out the stairwell's small window and saw flashing lights. I went outside to meet the police, who showed up within ten minutes after I did. I explained to the officer that Mom was off her medication and that she needed to go to the API. The police explained to me that they had received a disturbance call, and I confirmed to him that it was my mother. Another police unit showed up, and it was a police officer that I knew from having training with him in school. He was officer Mandalay. The first officer to arrive drove his vehicle onto the grass and parked directly in front of Mom's apartment. We walked upstairs, and the officer knocked on Mom's door to try to get her to open it, but she refused. The officer talked very kindly and calmly, trying to get her to open the door, but she still refused. Mom would open the door and look out but would then slam the door shut. I told the officer that I had a key, so I opened the door. The officer had to force his way into the front door, pushing the many clothes partially blocking the entry. The officer worked his way into Mom's apartment with another female officer. I continued to talk to Mom to keep her calm and to let her know everything was going to be fine. Both officers approached her slowly and calmly and began to put their hands on her to restrain her. Mom struggled a little bit with the officers, and they eventually had to handcuff her for everyone's safety. For the first time, I witnessed my mom as being extremely vulnerable, fragile, and weak. She could not fight them in the manner I had grown accustomed to seeing. My mother looked frail and tired. The officers walked her down three flights of stairs, and it was a struggle because Mom put up a little resistance. They made it to the police cruiser, and still it was a struggle trying to get her in the car. Right at the last surge to get her into the car, she spit in the face of the male officer who was not the one I knew. That really upset the officer, but he did not mistreat or manhandle her at all, although he did put a mask on her. I had never seen Mom spit on anyone, and when she did that, I knew she was not in a good state of mind.

The officer drove her to the API as I followed them. We made it to the API, and when we got there, Roger and Farrah were there waiting. The intake process to get her into the API was rough as well. Mom spoke negatively about Farrah, and then she said some really terrible things to me. It sort of hurt my feelings because she usually did not talk that way to me. Right in front of the API staff, the police officers, and Farrah and Roger, Mom said, "Frankie, you are a faggot, and you suck dick." A short time afterward, I just told Farrah, "I don't know how you deal with it, Farrah." Immediately she gave me a response that shocked me, "Mom knows what she is doing, and they can keep her in here for a long time for all I care." All the years of care and deep concern for Mom had been depleted from Farrah's bank of patience and willingness to show unconditional love. As Farrah and I witnessed her being transferred into the custody of the API personnel, we saw how Mom treated the API intake personnel like royalty and just walked down the hall with them as if nothing was wrong with her. We left the API and went home.

The very next day, I went over to Mom's apartment to check on her place, but before I stepped onto the stairs to go inside the building, I noticed some familiar items on the grass directly in front of where Mom's window was three flights up. The items were some of Mom's clothes and a F.E.D. summons with Mom's name on it. She was the defendant. An F.E.D. is a Forcible Entry and Detainer summons to remove a person from their living quarters. I knew exactly what the paperwork was because I was once a clerk for Alaska's court system. So now I knew what set Mom off, what triggered her to be uneased and got her stirred up. I immediately called Farrah and told her. The landlord had Mom served with that summons, and Mom did not know what to do. She was going to be kicked out of her home that she occupied for twenty-three years. Now I know a little bit about the law, procedures, statutes, and court proceedings because I worked at the state court system for twelve years, so when I saw the summons, I knew exactly what to do. The F.E.D. hearing was in just a few days, so Farrah and I needed to act fast. We came up with a plan to attend the hearing, and we did. We showed up in defense of our mother, and the landlord was there with the Anchorage Neighborhood Housing Apartment attorney. In the hearing, the landlord was trying to evict Mom in three days. Now it was my time to speak, and I told the judge that there was absolutely no way we could move all her belongings in three days. I explained that Mom had been in that apartment for twenty-three years and had lots of merchandise, plus we would have to clean the place. The judge agreed that we needed more time and gave us ten days to remove Mom's belongings. And that was what Farrah and I did with the help of Farrah's husband, her son, my daughter, and my girlfriend. It was a painstaking task, but we did it with a few days to spare. Mom had so much stuff that it filled a quarter of Farrah's backyard and half of her garage, and I took a lot of Mom's items as well and put it in my storage at U-Haul. The day after we finished moving Mom out of her apartment, I went to the API to tell her, and she was not pleased. Mom would not hear a word I had to say. She accused me and Farrah of getting her evicted from her apartment. I tried and tried to explain to her that the landlord filed paperwork to have her evicted for many reasons, like not paying her rent on time, not allowing her apartment to be inspected on a quarterly basis, damaging property, and threatening other tenants. But Mom refused to believe it, and for the first time that I ever remember, Mom did not like me.

Now our brother Ross who lived in Robust, Indiana, was playing a different role in this matter with Mom. For some time since Mom began seriously relapsing, all of us siblings were working together toward a common goal, and that was to help and assist her in any way we could. But now Ross was working against all of us, and we didn't know it. Mom had filled his head that we were mistreating her and got her evicted from her apartment. You see, our working together evolved around having conference calls so we could all discuss the well-being of Mom all at the same time. Ross lived in Indiana, Velvet and Wayne lived in Texas, and Farrah and I lived in Alaska, and the next scheduled conference call was different because Ross was talking differently. He was not on the same page as the rest of us when it came to Mom.

CHAPTER TWELVE

*Mom goes to live with Ross in Indiana, and
the family has absolutely no knowledge of the
travel; she has a catastrophic time there*

Mom was released from the API in September 2009, and we did not know where she was and where she might be living. We just knew she was released and had no home to go to, and she had not contacted me or Farrah. We were really concerned about her whereabouts mainly because we knew her history and condition, and if she was staying with someone, they may not know of her condition and could freak out if she had a mental relapse. Well a few months passed, and it was early 2010, and we had just found out where she was staying. Mom was in Robust, Indiana, living with Ross. Now everybody was in shock; we were really concerned and pissed off at the same time because Ross did not inform us that Mom would be living with him. We were concerned as to how Mom was going to receive help and assistance if she had a mental relapse. The way we found out was that Mom contacted Velvet to tell her that she had been staying at Ross's for quite a while now, and things weren't going too well. Remember, this was one of Mom's traits, calling family when she was about to go into one of her mental relapses. We set up a conference call to speak with Ross to discuss why he did not inform us that Mom would be living with him, and Ross's response was that we were mistreating Mom and that he could take better care of her. We asked him if he had done his homework as far as refilling her prescriptions and medication that she needed so that she could function normally, and then we asked if he found any mental health facilities there in case Mom needed to be admitted if she was to have another mental relapse. We also asked Ross if he considered forwarding Mom's disabilities benefits and retirement checks to make sure she got those things and could take care of herself. The answer to all those questions was a resounding "No." Ross explained to us all that he felt that Mom no longer needed medication and that the medication had poisoned her for years. He was going to pray over her, and God would heal her and cleanse her from using medication. Mom would now attend Ross's church, and he had get her involved in their worship and the whole church setting. When we heard this rundown of events, we almost went into a state of shock because we knew this could not happen and would not work. We were extremely mad at Ross and were in disbelief that he would do this. Farrah and I had dealt with Mom and her condition all our lives and had a great system on how to help her, and now Ross was moved by a few speeches that Mom gave him, and suddenly felt like he can change her. We felt sorry for Mom because we knew once she had a mental relapse, she would not be able to get the help she needed. We did not feel sorry for Ross for what he was about to go through. And wouldn't you know it, the shit would hit the fan.

Mom ran out of her medication, and her mental relapse was on and in full force. Things were quite bad for Ross and his family, and he did not know how to handle or deal with Mom and her condition. The next thing we knew, Ross had put Mom on a bus to go to Dallas, Texas, to live with Velvet without informing Velvet or getting her approval and having a plan in place. By now, we were livid with anger and disappointment with Ross. We were scramming to find out where she was. Mom finally made a call to Velvet, telling her that she made it somewhere in Tennessee, but she could not travel any further because she had run out of money. We called Ross and told him he needed to go get her as soon as possible because she had run out of money and was in some bus depot just sitting there. I can only assume that she really did not run out of money but that the bus driver put her off the bus because of her unusual behavior. Well, we found out that Ross traveled 489 miles to Tennessee to get Mom, and knowing Ross's behavior, I can assure you that he was mean to her when he found her. He drove her back to his house, and while she was there, things went badly until he sent her away. Ross's entire family was terrified by Mom's behavior because they had never seen anything like it before. We spoke to Ross once again, and he said that he would be putting Mom on a plane to come back to Alaska. He did not give us any specifics or anything but that he would be putting her on a plane back to Alaska. Now all we had to do was wait for Mom's arrival, but we did not have any information of her return at all.

About a month passed by, and Farrah heard that Mom was back in town and was staying with some white lady she met at the API. From Farrah's understanding, Mom and this lady were friends and got along well because they were in the same ward. The lady somehow found Farrah's phone number and contacted her and said that things were going well between her and Mom. Well about two weeks passed, and Farrah received a call from the lady at around 4:00 p.m. on a beautiful, sunny day. She was complaining about Mom's behavior. She gave Farrah the address, and went over to the house. My girlfriend Cassandra was with me, and she stayed in the car while we went into the apartment complex. Farrah, Roger, and I saw that the lady was staying in a secure building where we had to be buzzed in. We went upstairs, and the lady welcomed us into her apartment. She directed us to the bedroom, where Mom had locked herself. Mom was surely agitated and amped up, showing signs that she had gone into her mental relapse. Farrah, Roger, and I spoke to her through the door to try to get her to come out of the room, but she refused. Mom told us to leave her alone, and she talked about Farrah as if she was the devil. Mom was saying some pretty ugly things about Farrah, and it was not nice at all. Mom also brought up Farrah's daughter Sophia a lot, and that really irritated Farrah. She was having trouble focusing because of the mean things that were being said, especially since the lady was hearing these mean things and it was embarrassing. We decided to open the door by force by sticking a sharp object into the doorknob. We managed to unlock the door and force our way in. Mom was upset and started throwing things at us. Roger and I grabbed her and sort of forced her out into the living room, but she was being destructive and was threatening to destroy some of the lady's personal belongings in the house.

By now, the police were on their way because the lady was forced to call them, not knowing what to do. Well the police arrived, and once again, it was Officer Mandalay. He and his partner were so nice and patient with Mom. It is like God sent them to assist us. Per procedure, they must handcuff Mom, and they escorted her out to the patrol car. I waved to my girlfriend Cassandra to let her know that everything was all right. This was the first time that Cassandra saw my mother. What a way to be introduced to someone on their first meeting. Officer Mandalay got Mom into the patrol car, and he asked if she wouldn't mind searching her. I searched Mom's bra area, and she had about four BIC lighters in there. She had about six golden safety pins attached to her bra as well. I spoke to her softly and comfortingly as she let me remove her items. I told her I would keep them safe for her, and she agreed. I told her that I loved her very much and kissed her on the cheek, but right before she stepped into the police vehicle, she glanced over at Farrah as if she was disgusted with her. We followed behind the police patrol car to the API. The intake process now had changed a bit. The police officers were now directed to take Mom to Provision Hospital, where she can be evaluated to make sure she was mentally unstable. The nurse and staff then took some of Mom's blood, which was not an easy task, and that will determine if her medication was out of her system, which would give them a clear reading of her well-documented condition. We waited while that process was being done, and while we waited, Mom said a lot of negative things about Farrah. Mom was so amped up that the nurses had to strap her to the bed. Both Farrah and I tried to talk to Mom, but she ignored us both, especially Farrah. A few hours passed by, and the results came back, showing that Mom had no medication in her system. The doctor and nurse informed us that Mom would be transported over to the API. Once again, we watched her walk through the halls with the API staff workers as if nothing had happened.

I waited a few days to go visit Mom, and when I tried to check in, the receptionist behind the secure glass enclosure said that Mom did not want to see me. I was shocked because she had never done that to me before, so I left and did not return for about a week. This time, she did say that she would see visitors. I was let through the many secure doors, and I sat down waiting for Mom in the food court. She approached me and appeared to be angry. The first thing she said was that she was still angry with me for moving her out of her place, and then she said that she did not want to talk to me. I tried to explain, but she wouldn't listen. The visit was really short, and I left with Mom still angry with me. For the first time in dealing with Mom's condition, she and I did not see eye to eye. It was strange for me and quite disturbing. I went back to visit Mom about a week later, but she was gone. The API staff refused to tell me any information about her whereabouts.

CHAPTER THIRTEEN

*Mom returns to Alaska and lives in a local homeless
shelter and various hotels for a while*

Now that Mom had made it known that she did not want to
have anything to do with any of her kids, especially me and
Farrah, we struggled to find out where she was living. We
turned to our pastor, and he said that Mom was staying in a house that
was owned by the church, which was directly behind the church. The
house was about thirty yards from the church, but our pastor informed
us that Mom could only stay there a few nights at the most because the
house had already been leased out to someone else. After a few days,
we checked with the pastor again, and he said Mom had left and was
going to the homeless shelter, which was called the Brother Franklin
Shelter. It was located on the boundaries of downtown Anchorage, next
to a food shelter called Lentil's Café. Farrah and I drove to the shelter
to look for her, but we weren't allowed inside the facility, so we looked
through the window from the outside and saw no sign of her. We asked
someone in charge if they had seen Mom, and the person told us that
they kicked everyone out in the morning, and they can't come back
until it was time for bed, so we gave up our search for a few days and
lifted Mom up for prayer to the Lord. Farrah and I went back a few days
later around bedtime, and we tried to get into the shelter to speak with
someone to ask if they had seen Mom. They would not let us in again,

so Farrah and I looked really hard through the glass doors for about five minutes, and to our surprise, we spotted her. We saw her directly in front of us—it was at a distance, but it was her. She was surrounded by men as she made her pallet on the floor, but she looked happy and unafraid. The shelter was so crowded that they did not have any extra beds or mattresses, so the rest of the patrons had to make pallets on the cold floor. We watched her until she lay down and settled herself on the floor, and we walked away feeling proud of our Mom because she was surviving in such a tough environment. But we were sad because of where she was. Farrah and I checked back on her within that week, but the staff said she was gone because she had moved to a hotel somewhere downtown.

For several days, Farrah, Roger, and I drove around downtown searching for Mom with no luck until one day, I was passing the Everyone Inn bus depot, and guess who I saw sitting on a bench at the bus depot smoking a cigarette and looking very content? Our mother. I quickly parked down the street, got out of my car, and walked to her. I stepped up and stood right next to her with a small smile on my face, but my smile went away as quickly as it came because I could tell she was not happy to see me. I said hello to her, but she did not appear to be happy to see me. My thoughts were correct. Mom told me that she was still upset with me because I moved her out of her house, and now she was homeless. I continued to let her speak without interrupting her. She went on to say that she loved it right where she was because nobody messed with her. "You see, all these different types of people around me, they give respect to me and call me Mom. I give them advice, and they come to me for advice when they have questions. I sit here and smoke my cigarettes, and nobody bothers me. These cigarettes are my man since I don't have a husband or a boyfriend. Just leave me alone, son." Mom took another puff from her cigarette and blew it out toward me as if she shared with me her secret of survival, and I walked away. I was not afraid for my mom as I left her with the homeless, the misplaced, and the miscreants of downtown. I was more afraid of being downtown than Mom was, and I knew for a fact she would be all right because God would watch over her like he always had. That would be the last time

I would see Mom up close for a while, and that was around September 2011. I would drive through downtown every day in hopes of seeing her sitting on that same bench outside the bus depot, and some days I would see her as I passed by. I know Mom recognized my car because I would purposely slow down so she could see me drive by. She would not make any movements or even turn her head, pretending like she didn't see me, but I know she did. Some days when I would pass by and see her, I would blow my horn to let her know I see her, but she would not budge, wave, or even look in my direction. I didn't care as long as I knew I was checking on her, and I could feel in my spirit that she was happy, knowing I would drive by to check on her from time to time. I grew angry with Mom as time passed by, so I gave up trying to make amends with her. She was so adamant about believing that we moved her out of her place on purpose, so I just left her alone and let her be.

But on April 22, 2012, eight months since the last time I had spoken to my mother, once again God spoke to my spirit. God was telling me that I needed to go find my mother and speak with her. The spirit of God was too overwhelming for me to resist, so I went to my fiancée Cassandra and told her that I needed to go find and see my mother, and she totally agreed. Farrah had told me that Mom was staying at the Escalade Inn Hotel on the corner of C Street and Sixth Avenue, so we drove there and parked the car in the parking lot of the hotel. We walked up to the receptionist's window and asked the lady sitting inside the glass enclosure to page Mom and tell her that I was there to see her. The lady did page her, and she said yes, she would see me. The lady directed me and Cassandra to a commons area, and we sat down and waited. Mom walked down one flight of stairs looking just as strong and beautiful to me like she always had. I was so glad to see Mom, and the happiness was mutual. We hugged each other very hard and for a long time, and then I introduced her to Cassandra. Mom hugged her with the same force. We sat down and talked for almost an hour. During our talk, I noticed that Mom had a small lump above her left eye. It appeared to me that Mom had been in a fight. I asked her about the lump, and she said it was nothing. While we were sitting there, a young light-skinned black woman came downstairs to get some coffee and use the microwave. I knew this young black woman when I worked at a certain high school. She was a bad student, always getting into trouble. Mom looked at the young woman like she knew her and didn't approve of her. After the young woman went upstairs, I asked mom if she had been in a fight with her, and she said no. I took a picture of Mom, and we began to say our goodbyes. Mom said that she would like to see me again, and I told her that I would love that. We spoke about plans for the next time we would see each other, and then we said our goodbyes. I felt so good that I listened to God. I would see and stay in contact with her for the next two months. My relationship with my mom had improved so much that I was visiting her quite regularly. She even invited me to her hotel room. When I walked into her room, I thought I was looking at her apartment all over again. There were two beds in her room, but she only slept on the one farthest away from the door. She had lots of clothes on the other bed and had clothes hanging up. Her small refrigerator had a lot of food in it, and some had spoiled. It appeared that the room had not been cleaned for quite a long time. Mom even showed me her smoke room downstairs, which was the vending machine room. I would sit in there with her while she smoked, but I didn't care about her smoking or all the smoke as it filled the room because we were talking and having a good conversation. I wanted to spend every moment with her and be in every intricate part of what she was doing. Those were great times.

CHAPTER FOURTEEN

Miracle after miracle happens, yet sadly Mom
passes away on the day of her birth

It was now the third week of May 2012, and Cassandra and I got married at the state courthouse on May 25, 2012. It was a beautiful ceremony, with my best friend Franklin Carney being my best man and Cassandra's sister being her matron of honor. And to top that off, Cassandra and I closed on a house we purchased, and I tell you, the house was a miracle house from God. Cassandra and I were already living in a trailer we had purchased, but we needed more living space and wanted a bigger yard, so we had begun looking for a house to buy in March 2012. After a long search and looking after house after house, we found one. We liked it a lot, and it had a really big backyard with a nice front yard. The house had an upstairs and downstairs, with four bedrooms and two full baths. It was perfect. One problem was that the house was close to being foreclosed on, and if that happened, it would be difficult for us to get into the house, and the process could take a long time. Well we had our real estate agent put in an offer for the house, and we gave her an earnest check to show good faith, and then we waited. About a week passed by, and we got a reply on our offer. It sounded good, but I was not sure because I had done some recalculations of mine and Cassandra's finances, and on paper, it did not look sound enough that we could even afford the house, so I told our real estate agent that technically we could not afford the house and we would need to pull out of the deal. Well the sellers came back and said that they would drop the price of the house, and Cassandra and I talked about it and realized that we still could not afford the house. Our real estate agent went back and told the seller that, and they dropped the price of the house even further. At that point, the deal was too good, and we accepted the deal and closed on the house. I did whatever I could do to not accept that house, but I would find out later why God wanted us to have it. Cassandra and I soon moved into our new house, which was a task because we were working with a timeline, getting ready to go on our planned vacation to California, Mexico, and across a few states to Texas. We were scheduled to leave on June 25, 2012. Now that we were settled into our new house, I got a call from Mom saying she needed a place to stay for a few days while the hotel cleaned her room because they believed it had bedbugs, so Mom stayed with us for a couple of days. It was wonderful having her with us. She was a great guest, and her being there seemed like she belonged. I told her that we were getting ready to go on vacation and that we would like if she could stay in our house while we were gone, but she refused.

Well the two days passed, and Mom contacted the hotel management, but they told her that she was not welcome back to the hotel. The hotel management said that she brought bedbugs to the room and that the room and bed were infested with bedbugs. I tried to explain to the hotel management that they couldn't just kick my mother out like that without a thirty-day notice, but the manager didn't listen to me, so we got our pastor involved, and with his pull and status in the community, he convinced the management to let Mom return. She returned to her same hotel room with no problems, except management told Mom she had thirty days to find another place to live. We said that was a reasonable notice, but before ten days even passed, the management had kicked Mom out and had moved her items to another hotel. They had moved her to the Inlet Inn, and it was a run-down dump. They had placed Mom in a bottom floor room that was rat-infested and nasty, and the inn had lots of drunk people in and out its doors. The Inlet Inn would close down permanently after we moved Mom out. Farrah and I went and complained to the Escalade Inn management and asked them why they did not keep up with their side of the contract to let Mom stay there for the full thirty days, and they offered us no answer. We got the pastor involved once again, and the Escalade Inn management found her a second hotel to stay in. It was a little better, but not much. The place was called the Avenue Inn, and it had a lot of bad reviews on the Internet. I asked Velvet if she would look the Avenue Inn up on the Internet, and she saw numerous bad reviews and did not like the place at all. I went to visit Mom there, and she appeared to be okay, but I felt the place was not safe for her.

By now, June 25, 2012 had arrived, and it was time for Cassandra, the kids, and I to go on our vacation, so I told Mom goodbye and prayed for her. We left, and I did feel a little better and at peace about where Mom was staying. We would be gone for twenty-one days and would return on July 16, 2012. On July 17, 2012, I received a phone call from Farrah saying that Provision Hospital had called her, saying that Mom was there and that someone had found her on July 16 at the corner of Tennis Ball Street and Fifteenth Avenue, unconscious and without clothes from the waist down. Immediately we went to Provision Hospital. I was afraid I was going to see Mom in bad shape, but she wasn't. When I walked into her room, she said, "Hello, Frankie." It was such a relief to know she was alive and that she knew who I was. I asked her a few questions as to what happened to her, but she could not remember much. Farrah had walked into Mom's room at the same time that I did, but Mom did not welcome her. Farrah didn't appear all that excited to see her either, but I could tell she was glad that Mom was all right. Farrah also had one of her friends come to the hospital to pray with and over Mom, and Mom didn't seem too receptive to that, yet she tolerated and allowed it. There were several doctors coming to see her, and they were most interested in the bump over her left eye that I had noticed four months ago, when I had reestablished contact with her. Four months and that bump was still there? Now I was curious.

While she was unconscious, a doctor had removed a small portion of the tissue from that bump to get it tested to see if it was something to be alarmed about. I explained to the doctor that I first noticed the bump over Mom's eye on April 22, 2012, so we waited patiently for the result to return, and for the next five days, I would spend most of my time in the hospital with her, and we got along very well. On one of those days, I told Mom that I had married Cassandra, and she was ecstatic about that because she really liked Cassandra. I had Cassandra and her two kids come to the hospital with me to visit, and Cassandra's son Hagar, my new stepson, was so excited to go visit Mom, whom he didn't even know really. He warmed right up to her so easily that he even handfed her some of her meal, and Mom welcomed and liked it immensely. By now, two days had passed, and a doctor informed us that he had Mom's biopsy results, and it was not good, but the cure rate was high. The doctor told us that Mom had lymphoma in her head right above the eye and said it was the kind of cancer that was very treatable with an almost 100 percent curable rate. But he also informed us that lymphoma was very aggressive and that if Mom did not receive treatment almost immediately, she would have about six months to live. The doctor gave us that important information on July 25, 2012, which told us that Mom had until at least late December 2012 to live, so we needed to act fast.

We thanked the doctor, and Farrah and I immediately got on the conference call and informed the rest of the family of the diagnosis. For the most part, the five siblings were split on the decision for Mom to receive treatment. Mom rejected the idea of treatment at first, so we decided to deal with things in a priority manner. We had to fix Mom's living arrangements first, so I asked her if she wanted to come live with me and Cassandra. Mom was adamant about living on her own, but I told her that really was not an option anymore and that she would need some living assistance. Mom continued to show pride, so I just told her that she was coming to live with me and Cassandra, and her demeanor changed—she appeared relaxed, relieved, and excited about me putting my foot down in making that decision. It was easy for me and Cassandra since we had an extra room that she could stay in. Once I made that decision to have her live with us, I knew at that very moment that was why God wanted us to have that house. I had dreamed most of my adult life of buying Mom a house, but God made sure that we purchased that specific house so that Mom could live in a house that she could call her own. Looking back on it now, when I was putting up resistance to buying the house, it never occurred to me that it would be the last house on earth she would live in. It was so clear to me at that moment what God's purpose was for her. I used to pray and talk to God so often that I did not want Mom to die in her apartment alone, with me finding her days or weeks later after she had passed away. Once we had bought the house, I wanted Mom to die in our house—if that was to happen years later and was God's plan. God answered and honored my prayer and made sure she had a home of her own before she was to pass away. It came time for me to pick up Mom from the hospital and take her home, and it felt like she had lived with us for a long time. There was a greenhouse on the back deck, and she made herself right at home by going out there to smoke her cigarettes. She was in perfect peace with herself, and she simply loved it. There was a slide and swing set in the backyard, and she would go out there and smoke her cigarettes too. She was so content. It was fantastic and rewarding for me, and such a tremendous blessing of epic proportions.

Once we shared the information that Mom had cancer, Velvet heard the call from God and immediately booked a flight for herself and her son to come to Alaska so she could be with mom. A few weeks passed by, and Velvet and her son were in Alaska staying with us. Velvet was extremely instrumental in persuading Mom to change her mind about getting treatment for her cancer. Velvet, Mom, and I went to the cancer center to meet with doctors about the correct procedure to take because we needed to act fast, as the cancer was spreading quickly throughout Mom's head, and her face was starting to swell from the tumor enlarging. The doctor recommended chemotherapy, in which Mom needed to be fitted with a mesh mask. The process required Mom to have her face measured, and she needed to be stabilized while she took the chemotherapy so that the radiation could directly target just the cancer in her head and not affect anything else on her face like her eyes and brain. The doctor and other cancer treatment personnel gave us some advice on what to do so we could process the information, and they set the procedure within a couple of days. Mom had Medicaid insurance, and the insurance provided cab service for her to be picked up and take her to her treatment sessions. Everything was set and right on schedule. Well, Mom's first appointment came up, and the cab picked her up from the house and took her to the cancer center, and all I needed to do was to be there to pick her up. I went to pick Mom up at the expected time, and when I got there, she was already waiting outside, so she got in the car. I asked her how it went, and she said it went exceptionally well. Mom's next appointment would be in a week.

We went home and had a great time. Mom, Velvet, and I sat around and talked, laughed, ate fruit, and even got up to dance to music. Yes, Mom danced to one of her favorite songs, Paul Hardcastle's title song "Rain Forest." It was so cool, and for the next few days, we all had a great time. Mom had a lot of energy and was just so pleasant to be around, but because she was diagnosed with six months to live, hospice was ordered for her. Hospice set up a meal schedule that came with hot meals. They were dropped off at the house for Mom every other day. Cassandra and I were given the task of monitoring and administering all of Mom's medication, even giving her needleless shots in the mouth for pain if she needed it. It was a very easy and simple process, and a big plus was Cassandra was a certified nurse. A week passed by, and Mom had to go to her next chemotherapy appointment. Like clockwork, the cab picked her up, and all I needed to do was to be there to pick her up. When it came time for me to pick her up, and I went to get her, and she was sitting on a bench outside. I walked up to her and asked how the treatment went, and she gave a different response compared to the last response. Mom said she did not like it and that she was not going to go anymore. I walked out of the lobby area and got my car and drove up to the curb. When she got in the car, I said, "Mom, what happened?" She said that she did not want to talk about it, and I grew really concerned. We drove home in silence. When we got to the house, I tried again to talk to Mom, but she once again did not want to talk about it. I just said, "Well, Mom, you have an appointment next week, and maybe you will feel better by then." The next week came for Mom to go to her next chemotherapy appointment. By now, the cab arrangement had changed, and it would pick her up and bring her back home, so by the time I got off work and got home, Mom was already home, out on the back deck smoking a cigarette in the greenhouse. I asked her how her appointment went, and what she said to me next sent shockwaves through my body. Mom said, "God told me that I do not have cancer anymore and that I do not need to go to those chemotherapy appointments any longer." At that very moment, I knew something was wrong.

The next day, I went up to the cancer treatment center to speak with the doctor about Mom's progress, and once again I was in shock after what he told me. The doctor told me that Mom never showed up to take any chemotherapy sessions. I almost implied that the doctor was lying because I told him that I dropped her off the first time and even picked her up. And I told him that the cab had been bringing and picking her up and bringing her back home. The doctor told me that Mom never showed up and that she must come in to her next appointment, or they would cancel the rest of the treatment schedule and would not see her anymore because the cancer would have advanced too far to stop the spread and growth of the tumor. I immediately went home and spoke with Mom and told her what the doctor had told me. Mom said, "Son, when I went to that first chemotherapy session and they put that mask-shaping thing on my face, it was like they were putting death on me, and I could not move, so I yelled and screamed and told them to get that thing off me. I pulled the mask off me, and I ran out of there and into the lobby and sat down until you came to pick me up. The other times that the cab picked me up and dropped me off, I just sat in the lobby until the cab came back to pick me up. But son, God told me that I don't have cancer anymore." I just stood there with my jaw locked open and in shock and in confusion. For the first time, I felt real fear that I was going to lose my mother. It was becoming real what the doctor said that my mother was going to die within six months. I tried to explain to Mom what the doctor had said when she was in the hospital, of having six months to live. Then Mom spoke to me in a very soft, humbling voice and said, "Son, I am ready to go. I am tired, and I am ready to go be with the Lord." I wanted to cry, but I didn't because I knew I needed to be strong in front of Mom. I responded and said, "Okay, Maw." The next day, I called the doctor and hospice and told them that Mom did not want to continue with the treatment and that she was fine with her decision. Hospice told me that they would be by the house to give me and Cassandra more instructions and much-needed help as time went on.

It was August 28, 2012, Mom's birthday, and we all planned to get together at Applebee's, one of her favorite restaurants. We celebrated her seventieth birthday. That morning, I gave Mom a birthday card and wrote the number "70" in big numbers on the inside of her card. When she read it, she was shocked, and what she said also shocked me. Mom looked at the card and said, "Am I really seventy years old?" Mom slowly sat down in her recliner as if she was in shock as well and she said to me again, "Son, I am ready to go." And the first thing that came to my mind were some words she had spoken to me many times before over the course of our lives, which was a scripture from the Holy Bible, from Psalm 90:10, "The days of our years is threescore years and ten." I truly believe with all my heart that Mom remembered that passage of scripture by heart and was ready to go because she had lived what God had promised all of us, and that was what she had prayed for. Mom told me many times that she wanted to live to see her hair turn gray, and she did. Mom knew about suicide because that was what her dad did, committed murder-suicide. She told herself when she was a little girl that she would never ever commit suicide, nor ever talk about it. There were multiple times when Mom talked about suicide, but only to tell us kids that if any of us committed suicide, we would go straight to hell and would be with the devil for all eternity, and I truly believed that statement. Mom had set her own goals and desires, but she never knew she had made them and achieved them.

It was now the first week of September 2012, and Mom did something that I had seen many times before over the past forty years, but she also did something that I had never seen done within those same forty years. One night, around nine o'clock, Cassandra and I were sitting up in our bed talking and trying to wind down to go to sleep. We thought Mom was in her room preparing to go to bed as well, when suddenly Mom barged into our room and sort of yelled at us saying, "Stop talking about me!" And she went on to say, "Cassandra, you should know better to be treating me that way." Cassandra and I looked at each other in amazement, clueless as to what Mom was talking about, but I knew what was happening. I had seen this type of surprising behavior many times before. It was one of the signs Mom showed when she was getting sick or having an emotional breakdown, and I said to her in a soft voice, "Mom, no one is talking badly about you." Mom quickly turned around and went back to her room. About ten minutes passed by, and she came back looking very humble, and what she did next was something I had never experienced over the years. Mom said, "I am so sorry, Cassandra, son. Yelling at you that way was not necessary, and I apologize." Mom turned around and went back to her room. Like I said earlier, in all my times in dealing with Mom, she had never turned around and apologized so quickly. At that very moment, I knew Mom was different, and I felt like the growing tumor in her head was healing her mental perspective. Mom was different and seemed healed of her mental illness by the tumor, but I would be wrong as far as her health getting better from the cancer.

A couple of days after that apology, I saw her health decline right before my eyes. The first sign of that decline caught me off guard and sort of made me laugh, but I was unaware of what I was witnessing. Mom called me from her room, which was right across the hall, and said she needed help to the bathroom, so I went to help her. Mom stood up and started walking, but her steps were quick, shuffling baby steps. I thought she was playing with me because it was funny to watch, but I realized later that she was in the beginning stages of the cancer slowly shutting down her brain functions. A week later, Mom needed full assistance to go pee and take a bowel movement in the bathroom. A few days after that, she needed full assistance taking a shower, and I had to lift her up into the bathtub. Immediately I called my brothers and sisters and told them Mom's health was rapidly declining, just like the doctor said. By the beginning of the third week in September 2012, I had to order a wheelchair from hospice. Cassandra and I had to roll Mom around the house from her bedroom, to the bathroom, to the living room to watch television, and back. Farrah and I would talk about arrangements on how to best care for her, like bringing her meals and sitting with her, but I soon found out that Farrah was making plans with her own family on what was to take place in my house without consulting me and my wife. Who did she think she was, making plans in my house without discussing it with my wife and me? She was having her son, my nephew Ishmael, come to my house to bring Mom meals and soup and whatnot, but she never discussed the days and times with me and my wife. We never discussed who would be letting him in, as if I was going to leave my door unlocked, but I didn't put up too much resistance and said it was okay. But they were known for not arriving to places on time, and my nephew kept up the tradition and was not consistent in his commitment and time. A few days passed by, and there was no nephew to be found, so I canceled that plan and continued with hospice providing the meals and coming to sit with Mom. Within a few days, Wayne called me and told me he booked a flight to come to Alaska and would be here within two weeks. By now, Mom was just eating soup and drinking vanilla Ensure because she was not hungry. She really loved drinking vanilla Ensure. A few weeks passed by, and Wayne had arrived in Alaska, and he stayed with Farrah. Wayne did not come over to our house right away, probably because he didn't know what to expect and maybe because he was a little afraid. When he did come, he spoke and prayed with Mom. In total, Wayne only spent a few days with Mom before he had to go back to Texas.

After Wayne left, Mom's health really declined, and I ordered a hospital bed for her. It was brought over immediately and set up in her room. I set up a laptop on her bed and logged onto Skype so she and Velvet could talk. By now, Mom's speech was limited, and she couldn't speak too clearly, but Velvet understood her, and she enjoyed the Skype conversations. Cassandra and I were now putting Depends underpants on her because she was unable to get up and walk to the bathroom. Cassandra really took on the role of caregiver for Mom and would clean and change her Depends underpants and change her pants and clothes. Of course I assisted her, but it was strange seeing my mother naked when I was changing her clothes because she soiled them.

It was October 7, 2012, which was Farrah's birthday. Mom's condition was so bad that I thought that she would have passed away on Farrah's birthday, but I should have known that she was too stubborn to let that happen. Mom couldn't speak by that time, but if she could speak, I do not believe she would have wanted to pass away on Farrah's birthday. It was around October 13, 2012 now, and she was having trouble swallowing and even breathing, so I called to make a plea to Farrah and Roger to come see Mom because I believed she didn't have much time to live. As usual, they showed up a couple of days after I made the call. Farrah and Roger sang gospel songs for her, talked, and prayed with her. During the visit, Mom had a look on her face as if to say, "I know you're pretending to care for me, and I can't wait for you to leave me be." They spent over an hour with Mom, and I even joined in on the singing and praying, but the entire time Mom was not responsive to Farrah and Roger's singing, one-way conversations, and prayers. Mom was very much aware of what was going on and very alert of her surroundings. I could tell that she did not like the visit 100 percent. The next day, Farrah's kids came to the house to see Mom, and that went well.

It was October 17, 2012. I called Farrah and Roger to tell them that I believed Mom did not have much time left and that they better come over, and they quickly responded this time. Farrah, Roger, and their daughter Sophia arrived around 6:00 p.m., and we all went to Mom's room. They asked her how she was doing, and they say they loved her. I felt like they needed some privacy, so I left the room. They were alone with Mom for about ten minutes, and then suddenly they came out to the living room and began to put their shoes on to leave. They said their goodbyes to me and my family, and it appeared to me that they were hurrying. Maybe they were on their way to church or Bible study because it was a Wednesday, and Bible study was on Wednesday night. With that in mind, I wanted to go see Mom to make sure she was all right. Immediately I went into her room, and when I walked in and saw her, I was stunned. She looked like she was in a trance of some sort. Her eyes were popped wide open and just staring at the door, and then I looked down on a side table that was next to her bed and spotted her rings. Mom wore eight rings on her fingers and none on her thumbs, and I couldn't believe that the rings had been removed from her hands. I immediately knew Farrah had done it, and the surprising thing was that her husband Roger let her do that. Mom had worn rings like that for most of her adult life, and those rings were a source of comfort and security for Mom, and now she was vulnerable and hypothetically bare naked without her rings. Those rings weren't a source of power to her because she got her power and strength from the Lord, but they represented some of who she was. I told Mom, "Don't worry, I will fix this for you." I had a few photos of Mom on my cell phone that I took when she stayed with us for a few days when the hotel was cleaning her room, and I looked very closely at them and found some that showed Mom's hands and the rings locations on her hands. The positions were very clear, so I picked up the rings and placed them on the correct fingers the way she had them, and almost immediately, her demeanor changed and she fell asleep. I saw Mom relax, and she looked at me as if to say, "Thank you so much, dear son." I believe Mom would have spoken those words because in Mom's last few weeks before she couldn't speak anymore, whenever I did something for her, she would respond with the word of endearment "dear" at the end of her thank-yous. She was so grateful and appreciative for the things we did for her in her last weeks. I believe Mom was in total disbelief that Farrah would do that to her when she had lost the ability to ward off unwanted confrontations from Farrah. I immediately tried to call Farrah and Roger to ask them what made them stoop so low to remove Mom's rings from her hands, but they never answered their cell phones.

It was October 18, 2012, and Cassandra and I woke up early that morning at five o'clock to change Mom's Depend underpants and change her clothes before we go to work. We would give her water, make her an Ensure drink, and leave food next to her bedside even though she couldn't reach to get it, but you never know. By now, Mom was sleeping most of the time, so we felt like she would be just fine while we were away at work. My wife and I went on to work just like the previous days, thinking about Mom and her condition, but when I left the house to go to work on that morning of October 18, I felt Mom had many more days left, and it never occurred to me that the day was the eighteenth. It was 2:00 p.m. now, and it was time for Cassandra to get off work, so she came by the office to say bye, and I told her to let me know how Mom was doing when she got home. Cassandra left and made it home in about fifteen minutes. She opened the door and first went to our dog, which was a miniature chocolate toy poodle named Bow Wow. She let him outside to use the bathroom because he had been locked up in his kennel all day. Cassandra then went to the room to check on Mom, and she immediately called me crying to tell me to come home right now because she believed Mom was breathing her last breath. I urgently rushed home. Once I walked into Mom's room, she breathed her very last breath. I said to my wife, "Mom waited for us to get home so she could say her goodbyes, and I believe she didn't want to die alone." I cried and cried and kissed my beloved mother goodbye. I immediately called the rest of the family to tell them that Mom had passed away. When I told Farrah and Roger, they came over right away, and Roger cried very hard, but Farrah showed little emotion. When I called Wayne, he cried very hard over the phone, as did Velvet. When I spoke with Ross over the phone, he expressed a very subtle reaction. When I told my dad, his expression was one of discomfort, but it was controlled. I called Pastor Mayweather, and he came over and showed his respect. I then called the hospice nurse so she could come over to declare Mom's passing, and then the funeral director was called to pick up Mom's body. Farrah and Roger didn't even stay around for the funeral director to pick up her body because they had a church function to go to. It seemed to me that they just didn't give a damn. When the funeral director arrived, the atmosphere outside our house was simply and indescribably beautiful. The sun was setting behind the horizon, and it reflected off the roofs of our neighbor's homes and through the surrounding branches and leaves of trees. I couldn't feel any temperature outside because I couldn't tell if it was hot, warm, cold, or cool. It was the most perfect temperature. The director and his helper were dressed in a suit and tie when they came in, and they spoke softly with compassion. They then gently and lovingly handled her body, putting her in a beautiful royal burgundy body bag and then carrying her out to the Cadillac limousine hearse. As they drove away, I waved goodbye to my dear mother, and the scene was once again indescribable. They disappeared down the street like they were going to heaven. It was such a great scene that I was glad I witnessed it.

CHAPTER FIFTEEN

*Farrah's selfish, unbelievable, and shocking behavior
at Mom's funeral would divide the siblings forever*

N ow that Mom had passed, three siblings would have to make
flight reservations to fly back to Alaska to be a part of her
funeral. It will be Wayne's and Velvet's second trip within
the last few months, and Ross's first trip back since he left Alaska some
twenty years before. Mom's funeral would be on November 12, 2012,
and the arrangements needed to be made so Cassandra, Farrah, Roger,
the pastor, and I went to meet with the funeral director at the funeral
home. In that meeting, we agreed that every sibling would pay about
$1,000 each. Farrah and I also agreed on what would be engraved on
Mom's grave plate and what would be printed in the newspaper. Some
money was raised for Mom's funeral with the help of our cousin Fiona
Branch, which brought the split down to about $800 each. Wayne,
Velvet, and Ross did not have their portion, so I paid theirs, and they
promised to pay me back. Also, in the funeral arrangement meeting,
Farrah and Roger agreed to pay a certain portion as well, but I found out
later that they didn't. We had also agreed on a dress that Mom would
wear. Now in this book I will say something that I have not told anyone
about Mom's dress that she wore in the casket. In 2011, when Cassandra
and I lived in our trailer before we bought the house that God blessed
us with, I was going through some of Mom's clothes that we had taken

from her apartment about three years ago. I had about three or four large trash bags of her clothes, and one day while I was going through some of those clothes, I came across this beautiful turquoise dress that was the same color as Mom's birthstone. It was a beautiful dress. When I saw it, I truly believed that God wanted me to find that specific dress so that I could put Mom in it when she passed. I was just going through her clothes to straighten them up, not looking for that dress. It never occurred to me at the time that Mom would be dying anytime soon. And I found that dress long before I made up with Mom on April 24, 2012, the day that God told me to go find her and reconcile with her. That was the same day I saw her with that tumor over her left eye. When the family discussed what Mom was going wear in the casket, I told everyone that Mom and I had talked about that specific dress and that it would be the one that she would wear. Truthfully, Mom and I never discussed it. Like I said, I believe God wanted me to find that dress, and I had to do whatever it took to make sure Mom was dressed in it for her burial.

In preparing for the service, Velvet had called Farrah prior to coming back to Alaska to say that she had a poem that she wanted to read about Mom at the funeral service. Velvet read it to Farrah over the phone because she was in Texas, and they agreed at what segment of the funeral Velvet would read it. They also agreed to pass out informational fliers to some of the homeless people that Mom had contacted so they could be aware of Mom's passing and come to the funeral. All the siblings arrived back in Anchorage a few days before the funeral, but there was a problem. Once Velvet got here, she contacted Farrah so she could get together with her about handing out fliers to some of the homeless friends Mom was in contact with, but Farrah had already done it. Velvet was a little upset, but she didn't bother with it too much. It was a couple of days before the funeral, and we wanted to review the funeral program, but there was another problem. Farrah alone had given the okay for the program to be printed, but there was no place in the program for Velvet to read her poem. Now Velvet was upset, and she called Pastor Mayweather to try to get some help because Farrah was avoiding Velvet's calls. It was the day before the funeral, and the funeral director called us to say that we can come see Mom and how they prepared her makeup and clothing to see if it was satisfactory. Velvet and I went to the funeral parlor, and we walked into the room where they had her. From a distance, she simply looked beautiful, and it appeared that she was just asleep. Velvet and I looked at each other and said "Aw." Then we proceed to walk up to the casket to check out her clothing and her hands. We checked out her hands because Mom talked to us all for many years about how she wanted her hands positioned after she would pass. We looked at her, and we were in shock not about her hands but about her clothing. Mom was wearing a black skirt, a white blouse, and a black jacket. Velvet and I said to each other, "This is not what we gave the funeral director to put on Mom to wear." And we said to each other again, "Farrah had them change it." We immediately went to the director to tell him of our problem, and he said, "That is what your sister Farrah told us to put on her." I told the director that the other outfit was what our mother wanted us to put on her, and that was why we gave it to them. By now, we had discovered that Farrah and Roger had not paid their portion of the funeral payment, and I immediately went on and paid the entire bill. I informed the director of this development, and he agreed that since I paid, I had the right to demand the clothing change. He then instructed his staff, and she was rolled back to the dressing room area and changed into the outfit that we had given him the first time. Velvet and I went to the car and waited because we understood that Farrah and Roger were going to be coming back to the funeral home to view Mom. Like clockwork, Farrah and Roger came walking up. We watched them go into the funeral home. Velvet and I could only imagine what they were thinking and saying to themselves when they saw Mom in the other dress. Sadly to say, Velvet and I giggled a little bit about it. Shortly afterward, I called Wayne and Ross to tell them what happened, and they were in shock.

It was November 12, 2012, the day of the funeral, and we all gathered at the church and went over how the proceedings will progress, but suddenly, Farrah and Roger wanted to speak with the family, so we all went to a large room next to the main office. Farrah said, "I have good news." She told everybody that she did some research with Mom's former employer, the post office, and found that she had an insurance policy. Farrah was so happy and excited she almost couldn't contain herself. She went on to say that the policy had increased over the years, and everybody could get about five or six thousand dollars each. We were all looking at her in shock. Farrah asked us, "Aren't you happy that we are going to get some money?" Most of us just remained quiet, and then we walked out of the room and into the congregation area to start the funeral. The family sat down in the first two rows, and then Velvet whispered in my ear about the program, not seeing herself in it and having no space to say her poem. Velvet had already been to the pastor and Deaconess Bonner about placing her somewhere in the program, and they informed Velvet right before the funeral was to start that she would be able to read her poem at a certain part, and she did.

The eulogy had come to an end, and it was time for friends and visitors to come up to view Mom's body up close. Now it was the family's turn to come get one last close look and say their goodbyes. By now, all of the family had gone up and was saying their goodbyes and was standing just beyond the casket. I turned to look back at the casket, and just when I thought I could not be shocked any damn more, I was super shocked beyond belief again. I could not believe what I was seeing. Farrah was standing over the top of Mom's head and was taking all of her jewelry off. It was the most inexplicable and mean-spirited thing I had ever experienced in my life. We asked one another and the director what Farrah was doing, and he said, "Farrah wanted to remove the jewelry off your mother." I said, "Mom is supposed to be buried with whatever jewelry she was wearing." None of us wanted to cause any further scene than what was going on, so we didn't say anything. The entire family, church members, and visitors just stood around in disbelief. The casket was closed, and all of Mom's jewelry was in a ziplock bag in Farrah's hand. After that, a procession was formed, and we followed Mom's hearse to her final resting place at the Anchorage Memorial Cemetery.

A day later, we siblings called Farrah to ask her why she removed Mom's jewelry but received no response. But the next day, Farrah came to my house. Ross, Velvet, and Wayne were at my house filling out forms to apply for death benefits as Mom's beneficiaries from her job. I watched Farrah from my living room window walk slowly to my front door as if she was embarrassed and a shame. She rang the doorbell, handed me all of Mom's jewelry, and then turned around and left without saying a word. Roger was driving the car. We all continued to talk about Farrah's behavior and actions over the next few weeks, and we decided to set up a meeting with Pastor Mayweather to discuss them some more. We met with Pastor Mayweather to talk about the things that happened, but we got no resolution. Even though I participated in the meeting, I felt like I was in a lynch mob and we were going to lynch Farrah, but all we wanted were some answers as to why she behaved the way she did. I believe, and I can probably speak for my other siblings, that in my heart, I already knew the answer as to why Farrah behaved the way she did against Mom. Farrah never received approval or any admiration from Mom. Farrah could do no good in the eyes of Mom since she was a little girl. Mom let Farrah know that she did not approve or like most of anything she did. Farrah tried and tried, and no matter what Farrah did, it was never good enough. Farrah knew Mom was going to pass away, and she knew she would never get that approval or hear Mom say, "You have done a pretty good job, my oldest daughter." Therefore, Farrah saw the green light come on, and she took the only opportunity to let Mom have it. I also know that Farrah loved having the last word. Throughout Farrah's life, she made it a priority to always have the last word at everything we did. As kids eating at the dinner table, Farrah did her best to be the last one eating so she could brag in our face that she still had desert left after we all ate ours.

It was now August 2014, and surprisingly, Farrah tried to show honor to Mom by purchasing a grave marker for her grave site, but the kind gesture was not taken well by the rest of the siblings because she did not ask for our approval, input, or even our suggestions as to what quotes should be put on the marker. She just went ahead and purchased the grave marker on her own. One day, I just happened to visit Mom's grave site like I usually did, and my first reaction was of such glee and happiness to see a very nice grave marker in place of a small bronze one that came with the package that I paid for. But the glee and happiness was immediately dispelled when I saw what was on the grave marker, and it read as: "Amanda J. Rock," and written underneath Mom's name was "Farrah, Roger favorite son-in-law, Velvet, Wayne, Frankie." We siblings did not like it at all because our names were on the grave marker and because of my own personal belief—I didn't feel like it was right when the living had their names on a grave marker or a headstone. But I was even more shocked and dismayed that Ross's name was not on the maker. Regardless of the fact that Ross acted alone in bringing Mom to his house in Indiana, it did not warrant Farrah to leave his name off his mother's grave marker. I called the other siblings immediately, and they were all infuriated. I also called the pastor and the funeral director, and I was told a new grave marker would be ordered, but I had no idea what would be on it. A few months later, the new grave marker came, and the only change was that Ross's name was added. We siblings called Farrah once again to ask for explanations, and we received none. She never answered her cell phone. Now it has been over two years since Mom passed away, and we have not heard anything from Farrah, and all we have wanted to do is make attempts to get some answers.

Mom loved her some President Barak Obama and was so proud that he achieved his goal of making it to the highest office in the land as our United States President, and when he visited our city in June 2015, I went to Mom's grave site to tell her all about it. When our city's multiple media outlets started circulating pictures of him riding in his beautiful black armored limousine, I printed a copy and laminated it, and then I went to Mom's grave site and stuffed it in the opening of another grave marker that was placed on her gravesite. Almost immediately, I could hear Mom's voice like a spirit in the wind, just like the many times I heard her chant when she was alive, her voice very loud and with such pride and adoration of the man,

"O-ba-ma, O-ba-ma, O-ba-ma."

The Author's Personal Recommendations, Advice, and Suggestions

- You have a loved one with a mental illness disorder, in this case, paranoid personality disorder.
  - Make sure you receive a correct diagnosis of their disorder.
  - Notify your local police department and get the loved one on their city or community awareness list of the mentally ill. If there is not a list, talk with the department head to start one.
  - Inform certain neighbors, and leave them your number if you live at a different location.
  - Know the location of your nearest mental health facility and hospital.
  - Get a complete understanding of your loved one's disorder.
  - Know the medications they are taking. (If you can get that information, that is, because the loved one and the HIPAA laws might work against you.)

- When the loved one is showing early signs of unusual but familiar behaviors, know what those warning signs look and sound like. If their condition has reached this point, do not leave them. We did not have to worry about our loved one making death threats or suicidal threats.
  - If you are suspicious about their behavior, check on them.
  - Make multiple calls to certain family members far away and near.
  - Packages from family members may remain unopened.
  - They will purchase expensive items and not use them at all, and price tags will remain on the items.
  - They will slightly irritate their neighbors by talking to them through a closed door or by slamming their door to scare them to stop the neighbors from bothering them.
  - They will talk about Jesus Christ a lot.
  - They will talk and have two-way conversations with themselves.

- o Don't be surprised when they befriend someone outside the family and trust them over you.
- o They will go to their favorite store to return items for refunds.
- o They won't sleep.
- o They will be agitated.
- o Their voice will be hoarse.
- o Understand if the loved one is cognizant and sensible.

- When you know the loved one is deficient of their medication:
  - o Remain calm and don't act surprised at their behavior.
  - o Ask the loved one questions about their medication.
  - o Get family members involved either on a conference call, or meet where the loved one is.
  - o If you go to their house, make inconspicuous attempts to remove knives and potential weapons. Just make sure to turn them.
  - o Ask the loved one if you can take their trash out for them. There is something about trash that even your loved one will want to be rid of. They will like that you are willing to perform a task for them.
  - o If you all are in the same town/city/neighborhood, have all family members show up so that you can take turns interacting with the loved one because it can be exhausting.
  - o The family member who has a great rapport with the loved must enter their personal boundaries.
  - o The family member who has a great rapport with them must do the talking.
  - o There must be a balance of positive and negative in the loved one's presence/
  - o Continuously tell yourself you love them, no matter what.

- When you know the loved one must be assessed in order to enter the hospital:
    - Start making arrangements on how to get the loved one to the assessment process.
    - Contact your local police department to transport the loved one to be assessed. They have to handcuff them to protect the loved one in need.
    - Initiate small talk with other family members to take the loved one's mind off their surroundings.
    - Never threaten the loved one.
    - Ask questions that are not irritating and do not agitate.
    - Have a family member other than the great rapport member prepare an overnight bag of essentials that contain one or two sets of familiar clothes, undergarments, and lounge footwear.
    - Be extremely patient and understanding at this level of care. The loved one will not like going to the hospital.
    - Always be aware of your surroundings, and always protect yourself

- The transporting level of care
    - All family members go to the assessment.
    - Follow the transporting vehicle closely.
    - The family member with the great rapport must remain close.

- Things to do and not to do:
    - Other family members remain in the vicinity but layered away from the loved one showing mental deficiency.
    - Get assistance from as many family members as possible.
    - Set personal boundaries on how to help.
    - Be firm, not stern.
    - Know when to back down and away.
    - Make sure another family member is ready to pick the level of care.

○ Always protect yourself.

○ Talk positively at all times.

○ Talk about solutions.

○ Talk about family members the loved one may be fond of.

○ Never threaten the loved one.

○ Never be sarcastic or condescending.

- My final words of advice are please love and care for that loved one in spite of how they treat you and react to you. See the whole trial and tribulation through its entirety. Do not quit or give up on that person who desperately needs you. When you start a race, you must complete it. You start at the starting line, and you must finish at the finish line for these loved ones. My sister Farrah gave up on our mother as we were about to cross the finish line. At the end of our race with our mother, we were all tired, wary, and debilitated, but for me there was a great amount of achievement and success. In other words, I received my intrinsic reward because I did the best I could with the resources I had, and I finished the race with my mom. People may think badly about my father for giving up on his wife, but he had his breaking point, and he did the best that he could, and he still found time and made it his business to help us anytime we needed help with Mother. Farrah did all she could, and she had her breaking point too, but she tried to repay some of the damage she felt our mother gave her, and that negates all the work she put in. Some of the greatest advice I received from my father was to do your best and give all you got, so if you must walk away, you will have no regrets. I have peace of mind, but I do have one, maybe two regrets, that I wish to not say at this moment.

Mom, I know you are looking down on me from heaven, and I dedicate this book to you and your legacy. I also write to help others. I love you so very much with all my heart. Amanda Jean Rock, my mother, I miss you oh so much.

My Conclusion, Final Words, HIPAA Law, and Disclosure

I disclose that I am not an expert, a clinician, a doctor, a psychiatrist, a psychologist, a professional therapist, or a mental illness doctor. This book is true and accurate recalled to the best of my ability from actual events in my life. Only the prelude theory is fabricated from a theory of mine, and that was based actual events and theorized to fill in the lost and never-told events. I have expressed my opinions based on my many years of experience. Use my advice at your discretion.

This memoir is about my mother's mental illness and how it affected our family. Even with all our challenges in life, we continue to move forward. As normal as life appeared to me and for people outside our family, life really was not normal. Growing up in a home with a mentally ill parent, especially a loving mother, things always seemed a little different for me, but normal enough not to be alarmed or tell someone outside our family. But as I got older, I realized how different our family was from other families. In life as an adult, I would truly see how different things were from other families. As a preteen and getting older, from my perspective, life was scary, strange, unpredictable, and uncertain, but it felt normal because we didn't know anything else. Some might say that my dad didn't care because he didn't think or maybe felt like we didn't need counseling. Dad probably just wasn't aware that we needed help because we appeared to be normal. As I look back on my life now, I really wish we could have received counseling. I have two brothers and two sisters who went through the same mental illness experience as I did, and none of us are drug addicts, alcoholics, or criminals, but I can tell you we are all not completely right mentally. I have been married multiple times; Farrah appears to be clinically depressed but won't get help; Ross isolates himself from his own immediate family and leads us to believe that he does not like us and is deeply into a religion that is unknown to us; Velvet can't be satisfied in a relationship and actually hinders her only son's growth by protecting him; and Wayne, who should have been the most successful out of all of us, can't seem to find himself. So my advice for anyone who has a loved one who has a mental illness, you must seek counseling because the effects of mental illness also affects everyone involved. In dealing with a loved one who has a mental condition, you must be patient and have an understanding that reaches beyond understanding because the loved one with the mental illness will do things that will challenge your comprehension, understanding, and logic. You will ask yourself many times, "Why are they doing this? And why did they do that?" In our case, our mother would be so normal at times, and then suddenly her mental state would change. There are mentally ill people who do not go back and forth in their behavior. Your love for the mentally ill person will be tested beyond your unconditional care and concern, and you would wonder how you would behave in normal circumstances. If you have a mentally ill loved one, you must learn and completely understand the difference between normal and abnormal behavior to properly deal with it. A loved one can be so hard to understand because you look at yourself and know how your mind works, and you ask yourself, "How is it that their mind is different from my mind?" My mother had a chemical imbalance in her brain. She lacked a certain self-producing chemical, and she needed to take a certain medication to make her brain normal. When she ran out of that medication and it was out of her system, she would do things that were not normal. Mom was not able to control her behavior on her own and therefore needed a certain medication to do that for her. That puzzled me, and I just could not comprehend that fact, but I do fully understand that my mother needed help during those times when her medication was out of her system. And because of my love and care for her, I could maintain a high level of patience and understanding. When I was ten years old, I wanted to help my mother so badly that I used to pray that whatever was in her that caused her to behave that way, I wanted it to come into me instead.

The word *crazy* is such a terrible and uninformed word that should be banned from ever being used in normal or casual conversation. People in the church my mother used to attend used to say she was crazy, and I knew that was not true. This is my mother you are talking about, and I know her, and she is not crazy. She is the sweetest and dearest lady I have ever known, and had you really gotten to know her and look beyond her mistakes that she had no control of, you would know her and you would come to love her the way I did and still do. I want to tell these people that she has a chemical imbalance, but I know they will not understand because all they see is this untimely, infrequent, and unknown reaction that probably scares them and their perception. I even used to call people crazy for the same uninformed reasons, but I don't call people crazy anymore, and I try to stop others from using that word because most people really don't know what crazy is. Just because a person doesn't act the way everyone else thinks they should, it does not mean they are crazy.

Some doctors diagnosed my mother as having only bipolar disorder in her early years, and she kept that label for many years. Bipolar Disorder is a psychological condition in which a person goes through mood swings. There are periods of depression and periods of mania. Symptoms of depression include sadness, fatigue, feelings of worthlessness, and thoughts of death or suicide. Symptoms of mania include high energy levels, promiscuity, high self-esteem, poor judgment, little temper control and reckless behavior. This is according to www.goodrx.com. I do not ever remember my mother being depressed or having euphoria which is associated with bipolar disorder. I never saw bouts of, nor heard her speak of, hopelessness or despair. Another definition of depression from Merriam-Webster dictionary is "a state of feeling sad; may be

133

described as feeling sad, blue, unhappy, miserable, or down in the dumps. An illness that involves the body, mood, and thoughts; can also affect the way a person eats, sleeps, feels about himself or herself, and thinks about things." My mother talked a lot about living. She talked a lot about living old enough to see her hair turn gray and had hopes of getting back together with my dad, her ex-husband, up until the day she died. Mom loved getting up on Sunday mornings to go to church. Mom frowned upon suicide and told us kids about it, saying that we would go to hell and spend eternity with Satan if we killed ourselves.

Depression disorder affects my sister Farrah, but she won't get help as far as I know. She would hibernate in her bedroom many times when my family and I would come over to visit her, and she would not get out of her bed. This happened too many times for me to count.

My mother's mental state was misdiagnosed for many years. The first effective and helpful drug that I ever remember my mother using was a drug called lithium. It made her sleep for long periods of time, and a key component to staying well mentally is getting plenty of rest and sleep, and Mom got a lot of sleep. Mom would sleep from ten to twenty hours a day, only getting up to use the bathroom and get something to eat. When a person sleeps, the brain/mind rests, but when the brain/mind does not sleep, stress compounds. Stress is like a branch that reaches far and extends into other areas of a person's life. Mom used to worry about so many different things that she couldn't give her mind the proper rest it needed. I know Mom took a combination of other drugs that helped her as well, besides the lithium, but after so many years, the lithium no longer worked. My advice to anyone with a loved one or loved ones with mental disabilities of any kind, is to know the symptoms they are displaying or showing. And please, please get a second opinion because with my forty-plus years of experience in dealing with doctors, some care more than others, and some spend more time really wanting to find out what is ailing your loved one or family member so that they can receive the proper diagnosis and the correct help they need. If that loved one or family member takes medication that is incorrect, they may show a behavior or symptoms that are false and incorrect. My mother took a cocktail of different drugs that no doubt hurt her in many ways. She was dysfunctional and despondent most of the time with the family. Mom virtually had no relationship with most of her grandchildren because she was, for lack of a better word, comatose. The definition for comatose is "lethargic, exhausted, sleepy, inert, sluggish, and inactive." I believe Mom truly wanted to have a relationship with her grandchildren, but the medication rendered her despondent. She was extremely adamant about getting her rest and sleep because she hated going into the hospital's psychiatric ward for her ailment, as going there was like going to jail or prison—it took her freedom away. My mother died October 18, 2012, and as of January 26, 2017, I finally found out the real diagnosis of her condition, and it was *paranoid personality disorder*.

I was searching online and found this: "The specific cause of this disorder is unknown. It appears to be more common in families with psychotic disorders such as schizophrenia and delusional disorder, which suggest that genes may be involved. Paranoid personality disorder can result from negative childhood experiences fostered by a threatening domestic atmosphere. It is prompted by extreme and unfounded parental rage and/or condescending parental influence that cultivate profound child insecurities. The *symptoms* of this disorder are suspicion, concern with hidden motives, expectations to be exploited by others, inability to collaborate, social isolation, poor self-image, detachment, and hostility" (from www.psychologytoday.com/conditions/paranoid-personality-disorder). I disagree with poor self-image and hostility. Mom was the nicest dressed lady around, and she purchased the most expensive clothing and items from some of the most expensive stores she could find until her money could not afford it. But she will still do whatever she could do to buy expensive items. I also disagree with hostility because it is a strong word that didn't apply to Mom until the last few years of her life. The definition of hostility is "hostile behavior, unfriendliness, or opposition. A state of ill will and bad feeling." Mom exhibited that type of behavior in her later years. In her early and middle years, she was just short and direct with certain people. She would be short and straight to the point if she didn't want to be patient with you. Later in life, she was hostile and displayed some physical aggression toward just about anyone. As long as medication was in her system, she was the greatest and kindest lady you would ever want to meet, and that was how she was in her last days.

The HIPAA laws. Years ago, before the HIPAA Privacy Rule went into effect, patients couldn't leave when they wanted to. They were locked away for long periods of time, and a lot of the times they were only released at their family's discretion per a court order or of a doctor. The HIPAA is the Health Insurance Portability and Accountability Act, which is a federal law that gives you rights over your health information and sets rules and limits on who can look at and receive your health information.

Summary of the HIPAA Privacy Rule: (I took this information from www.caringinfo.org.)

HIPAA is a federal law that gives you rights over your health information and sets rules and limits on who can look at and receive your health information.

Your Rights

You have the right to

- Ask to see and get a copy of your health records.
- Have corrections added to your health information.
- Receive a notice that tells you how your health information may be used and shared.
- Decide if you want to give your permission before your health information can be used or shared for certain purposes, such as marketing.
- Get a report on when and why your health information was shared for certain purposes.
- If you believe your rights are being denied or your health information isn't being protected, you can
  - File a complaint with your provider or health insurer, or
  - File a complaint with the U.S. government.

You also have the right to ask your provider or health insurer questions about your rights. You also can learn more about your rights, including how to file a complaint form, on the website www.hhs.gov/ocr/hipaa/, or by calling 1-866-627-7748.

Who Must Follow this Law?

- Doctors, nurses, pharmacies, hospitals, clinics, nursing homes, and many other health care providers.

- Health insurance companies, HMOs, and most employer group health plans.
- Certain government programs that pay for health care, such as Medicare and Medicaid.

What Information Is Protected?

- Information your doctors, nurses, and other health care providers put in your medical record.
- Conversations your doctor has had about your care or treatment with nurses and other health care professionals.
- Information about you in your health insurer's computer system.
- Billing information about you from your clinic/health care provider.
- Most other health information about you, held by those who must follow this law.
  (c) 2009 NHPCO.

Summary of the HIPAA Privacy Rule (continued)

Providers and health insurers who are required to follow this law must keep their information private by

- Teaching the people who work for them how their information may and may not be used and shared.
- Taking appropriate and reasonable steps to keep your health information secure. To make sure that your information is protected in a way that does not interfere with your health care, your information can be used and shared
  - For your treatment and care coordination;
  - To pay doctors and hospitals for your health care;
  - With your family, relatives, friends, or others you identify to be involved with your health care or your health care bills, unless you object;

- To protect the public's health, such as reporting when the flu is in your area; or
- To make required reports to the police, such as reporting gunshot wounds. Your health information cannot be used or shared without your written permission unless this law allows it. For example, without your authorization, your provider generally cannot
  - Give your information to your employer,
  - Use or share your information for marketing or advertising purposes, or
  - Share private notes about your mental health counseling sessions.

CPSIA information can be obtained
at www.ICGtesting.com
Printed in the USA
LVOW11s0825170717
541425LV00001B/55/P